THE ADVANCEMENT OF LEARNING

Building the Teaching Commons

Mary Taylor Huber

Pat Hutchings

○

Foreword by

Lee S. Shulman

THE CARNEGIE FOUNDATION FOR THE ADVANCEMENT OF TEACHING

A Carnegie Foundation Report on the Scholarship of Teaching and Learning in Higher Education

JOSSEY-BASS
A Wiley Imprint
www.josseybass.com

Published by Jossey-Bass
A Wiley Imprint
989 Market Street, San Francisco, CA 94103-1741 www.josseybass.com

Library of Congress Cataloging-in-Publication Data
Huber, Mary Taylor, 1944-
The advancement of learning : building the teaching commons / Mary Taylor Huber, Pat Hutchings ; foreword by Lee S. Shulman.
p. cm.
Includes bibliographical references and index.
ISBN-13: 978-0-7879-8115-0 (alk. paper)
ISBN-10: 0-7879-8115-X (alk. paper)
1. College teaching. 2. Action research in education. I. Hutchings, Pat. II. Title.
LB2331.H85 2005
378.1'2—dc22 2005012459

Printed in the United States of America
FIRST EDITION
HB Printing 10 9 8 7 6 5 4 3 2 1

CONTENTS

The Carnegie Foundation for the Advancement of Teaching

Founded by Andrew Carnegie in 1905 and chartered in 1906 by an Act of Congress, The Carnegie Foundation for the Advancement of Teaching is an independent policy and research center whose charge is "to do and perform all things necessary to encourage, uphold, and dignify the profession of the teacher and the cause of higher education."

The Foundation is a major national and international center for research and policy studies about teaching. Its mission is to address the hardest problems faced in teaching in public schools, colleges, and universities—that is, how to succeed in the classroom, how to best achieve lasting student learning, and how to assess the impact of teaching on students.

FOREWORD

I SPENT EIGHT YEARS as an undergraduate and graduate student at the University of Chicago in the 1950s and 1960s. My memory of the institution is organized around people and places—the individuals whose teaching and being inspired my ideas and commitments, and the settings in which those acts of learning and development took place. And no setting represents the intellectual and personal richness of the place more than a space on the first floor of Judd Hall, the Judd Commons rooms. In those rooms we drank coffee or tea each morning and each afternoon. Faculty members and students gathered together and exchanged ideas and gossip, tough criticisms, and good yarns. It was one of the things that made life at Chicago so rich and rewarding.

But it was only when I moved on to my first teaching position as a newly minted, full-fledged Ph.D. that I discovered just how special life in that Commons rooms had been. Working with students was wonderful. But when it came to colleagues, the classroom turned out to be a lonely place, an experience (as I have written elsewhere) of pedagogical solitude. As researchers, my colleagues and I had energetic interactions, both within the institution and across institutional boundaries. The teaching life, however, was a private experience.

As Mary Huber and Pat Hutchings make clear in this volume, that unhappy situation has begun to change. Teaching and learning are now, increasingly, a focus for conversation among faculty, and the subject of lively intellectual exchange. New places and occasions to talk about pedagogy are springing up; new outlets for written work are appearing; and experimentation with multimedia representations of teaching and learning is thriving. And through all this activity, a commons for teaching is emerging that is just as vibrant as the one I experienced in Judd Hall as a graduate student.

As many of you know, the scholarship of teaching and learning is a major theme of the Carnegie Foundation, one that has been central to our work for some time, going back to *Scholarship Reconsidered* and *Scholarship Assessed,* and beyond. Building on Ernest Boyer's work and his collaborations with Gene Rice, Mary Huber, and others, I see it as one of the

Foundation's most important continuing legacies. The Carnegie Academy for the Scholarship of Teaching and Learning (which we call CASTL) has been our special program in this area, but the habits, values, and commitments of such work—what Huber and Hutchings describe as the movement's "big ideas"—run through all of Carnegie's projects, whether undergraduate, K–12, or graduate and professional education. The scholarship of teaching and learning invites faculty at all these levels to take teaching seriously as intellectual work, ask good questions about their students' learning, seek evidence in their classrooms that can be used to improve practice, and make this work public so that others can critique it, build on it, and contribute to the wider teaching commons.

It may be interesting to contrast this current emphasis in Carnegie's work with an important theme from the foundation's historical legacy—and it is one that characterizes much of the current policy climate, as well. Beginning with the Flexner Report in the period of 1908 to 1910, the foundation pioneered the external investigation, review, and evaluation of the work of higher education. Employing teams of outside experts, the foundation conducted incisive studies of the quality of education in the professions and in undergraduate programs, even on the impact of intercollegiate sports on the quality of collegiate education. This work prefigured the current climate of accountability and external oversight of the work of our educational institutions. However, in later years, the foundation began to communicate a very different message. The role of educational leaders was not merely to respond to external evaluations of their efforts. Instead, as *Scholarship Reconsidered* made clear, the professional responsibility of educators was to engage continuously in their own efforts to study the quality of their work, its fidelity to their missions, and its impact on students intellectually, practically, and morally.

Those of us who have been involved in this work have big ambitions for it: to build knowledge about teaching and learning in the classroom; to transform our educational institutions so that they support and encourage a scholarly approach to improvement; to invent new forms of documentation that better represent the intellectual work of teaching; to develop models of classroom inquiry that balance concreteness with the possibility of generalization; and to advance visions of what's possible for student learning that matters. These are important ambitions and they are, of course, among the reasons that the Carnegie Foundation has been so dedicated to this work.

But I would like to propose what may at first sound like a less grand ambition as well—and I make it with campus leaders especially in mind.

Taking a page from the work of Richard Elmore at Harvard, I propose that to "scale up" the scholarship of teaching and learning, we need to look for ways to "scale down." The challenge to campus leaders, then, is to find ways to plant the seeds for a teaching commons in their own institutional settings. This may not, at first, entail the kind of radical change implied by the language of systemic reform; as my colleagues make clear, it may begin with a small group of individuals who can show the way, a few departments where the climate is right, a few powerful, focused conversations that, by their intellectual sparkle and pragmatic promise, draw others in as well. But all of these need the support of campus leaders.

This support often takes quite small forms as well as large ones: setting aside spaces where faculty from within and across fields can convene and exchange ideas and practices—spaces that are perceived as centers for scholarship and not as emergency rooms for troubled teachers; providing modest budgets for food and drink that can nurture the bodies as well as the souls of participants; finding ways to make the collaborative intellectual and creative work of team teaching an attractive option; providing recognition and reward for scholars of teaching that are comparable to those afforded more traditional scholars; setting the expectation that teachers gather evidence of their students' learning that goes beyond the students' responses to end-of-course evaluations.

I make this plea to college and university leaders having visited more campuses than I can count over the past seven years, almost always in one way or another to talk about the scholarship of teaching and learning. The variety of places is notable: Princeton University, Wabash College, Ohio State University, Mills College, Foothill (community) College, Messiah College, Youngstown State University, and Columbia College in Chicago (where I go next week), to name just a few. In all of my travels, I have been struck by the level of interest in this movement and also by the power of small changes that begin to add up in truly consequential ways. The challenge for campus leaders now is to make a firmer place for such changes, to tap into and sustain the groundswell of interest, and give it institutional shape. This is not simply the right thing to do; it's the smart thing. As this volume documents, the scholarship of teaching and learning brings real benefits for students, signals institutional commitments to learning, helps meet calls for accountability, and provides authentic classroom-based evidence to meet new accreditation standards.

But not all of the benefits are institutional, as I am reminded by Carnegie's now 100-year-old mission "to do and perform all things necessary to encourage, uphold, and dignify the profession of the teacher and the cause of higher education." What comes through most clearly in this volume is the power of the scholarship of teaching and learning for teachers themselves. To see one's professional life through these new lenses is an energizing experience, one that changes teaching—the major component of most faculty's work—from a private to a public endeavor.

What Huber and Hutchings have done so well is to capture not only the large contours of the movement (what it has achieved as well as its future challenges) but the human side of this work: what it means to teachers to have colleagues, to see in teaching exciting questions, to engage with the teaching commons in ways that are as yet *un*common, but which are already beginning to change the pedagogical culture of higher education. With imagination, leadership, and luck, the Judd Halls of the future will be places of intellectual and personal richness for scholars, not only in their capacity as researchers, but as teachers as well.

Lee S. Shulman
STANFORD, CALIFORNIA
AUGUST 2005

PREFACE

SOME FOUR HUNDRED YEARS AGO, in a book entitled *The Advancement of Learning,* Sir Francis Bacon made an eloquent argument for the value of empirical inquiry into workings of the natural world. Thanks to Bacon and his many distinguished successors, this argument no longer needs to be made for the sciences—or for many other fields of study. Today, that impulse continues to extend into new areas of work and life. In this book, for which we have borrowed Bacon's felicitous title, we report on a movement that is bringing a commitment to observation and inquiry to the task of teaching in higher education. In particular, we look at how a scholarship of teaching and learning is developing among college and university faculty as a way of improving the education of students in their own classrooms, institutions, disciplines, professions, and fields.

There are many ways to improve the quality of higher education, but we believe that the scholarship of teaching and learning holds special promise. Watching the movement gain momentum over recent years, we have been struck by the power that comes with seeing teaching as challenging, intellectual work—work that poses interesting, consequential questions. The scholarship of teaching and learning invites faculty from all disciplines and fields to identify and explore those questions in their own teaching—and, especially, in their students' learning—and to do so in ways that are shared with colleagues who can build on new insights. In this way, such work has the potential to transform higher education by making the private work of the classroom visible, talked about, studied, built upon, and valued—conditions for ongoing improvement in any enterprise.

This transformation in the culture of college teaching is, as we see it, the goal of the scholarship of teaching and learning, and in this book we describe both the progress toward that goal and the challenges that must be met if this movement is to deliver on its promises. We look, therefore, not only at the scholarship of teaching and learning narrowly construed but at the larger terrain. In this *teaching commons,* as we call it, communities of educators committed to pedagogical inquiry and innovation come together to exchange ideas about teaching and learning, and use them to meet the challenges of educating students for personal, professional, and civic life in the twenty-first century. All who are committed to this teaching mission, we conclude, must seek ways to make new pedagogical practices, tools, and understandings broadly available, not only by building the teaching commons but also by protecting it and ensuring access.

The argument that teaching, when conducted with systematic attention to learning, might be considered a form of scholarship has been provocative for many, and we are aware that readers bring different types and levels of engagement with the topic. Some will come to this volume with extensive experience in pedagogical research—work that predates and lays the groundwork for today's scholarship of teaching and learning movement. Others will come as recent entrants into the field, excited about the experience of looking systematically at their own classrooms but with questions, and concerns too, about the prospects for such work and how to make a place for it on already heaping academic plates.

Faculty will, we suspect, constitute the biggest audience, and that is good news because the involvement of "regular" faculty from across a full range of disciplines and fields is a sine qua non of this work. But the scholarship of teaching and learning cannot thrive without leadership from presidents, provosts, deans, and department chairs, and so we have also endeavored to write a book that speaks to academic administrators who may know of the topic but not be clear about its implications for their own institutional context, or how best to harness and advance its promise.

With this range of readers in mind, we have done our best to avoid jargon, to provide a diverse set of examples, and to answer the questions a wide (and busy) audience is most likely to have: What is the scholarship of teaching and learning? What traditions does it build on? What are its distinctive claims and possibilities, its "soft spots," its successes and results, and its implications for academic culture and careers? Our aim is not to promote a specific model of the scholarship of teaching and learning, or to provide technical guidance for those seeking to do such work, but to place our topic in a broad landscape of efforts to bring greater prominence to the work of teaching. Our approach is primarily descriptive but we have not been hesitant to express our own values and commitments, and to convey our own sense of the most promising directions for the future.

Organization of the Book

The scholarship of teaching and learning cannot be understood without a sense of its history, and it is there that we begin in Chapter One. Pedagogy is not a new subject, and teaching's aims, methods, and material culture have gone through several significant transitions over the last several hundred years. But something is different today. Teaching is complicated in ways it arguably was not in earlier periods. New students, new technologies, new ideas about learning itself and about the goals of education are changing the classroom, bringing challenges and even frustrations but also unprecedented waves of innovation and experimentation. This is where the scholarship of teaching and learning enters the scene, as a response to shifting conditions.

Chapter Two takes up the task of definition. Because the scholarship of teaching and learning assumes different forms in different contexts (disciplines matter a lot, for instance), and because it is still evolving, a single, simple definition misses much of what is important. But now, some fifteen years after its introduction in the influential Carnegie Foundation report *Scholarship Reconsidered* (Boyer, 1990), it is important to be clear about the rationale for this work and the elements it comprises. What needs does it serve? What makes it different from "just plain" good teaching? And what does it promise for the improvement of learning? These are the questions we address in Chapter Two—and then elaborate on throughout the volume.

In Chapter Three, the camera moves in closer, looking at examples of the scholarship of teaching and learning—projects from a range of fields and settings exploring a variety of questions and issues. The examples are, we believe, tantalizing in themselves, but in addition they suggest possible themes and crosscutting elements that can serve as signposts and markers for mapping the commons in ways that allow users to navigate and tap into it. Along the way the examples also provide further, more concrete illustrations of what the scholarship of teaching and learning can offer to those who invest time and resources in the work.

Chapters Four and Five function as a pair, examining two important contexts for the scholarship of teaching and learning. The former charts the pathways that take faculty into this work: what prompts them to become involved, the communities they encounter and engage with in the process, and some of the obstacles along the way. Chapter Five then turns to campus developments that support the scholarship of teaching and learning, looking at evidence and examples of the new communities, structures, and policies that are needed. Looking through the lens of the commons, we see real progress on campuses, though certainly there are plenty of further challenges as well. The scholarship of teaching and learning is a long-term agenda, and it will take energy and leadership to achieve its promise.

Chapter Six brings us to the important epistemological issues that arise around the scholarship of teaching and learning. Picking up on themes introduced in Chapters Two and Three, we explore in more depth what it means to build knowledge through the scholarship of teaching and learning, for that, after all, is its claim: not only to improve the work of its practitioners but also to contribute to a larger body of knowledge. What is the character of this knowledge, and in what ways can it be both a significant and useful contribution to the commons? What forms does it take now, and what possibilities do new media offer for its representation? How can the quality of this kind of work be judged?

Finally, Chapter Seven looks at what needs to be done to support and sustain the scholarship of teaching and learning as a way for faculty and their students to contribute to and benefit from the teaching commons. We begin by looking at the experience of students in classrooms where the scholarship of teaching and learning is being practiced, and how that work helps students become more intentional, purposeful, lifelong learners. This is good news for students, of course, but being smarter about learning is important for all of us today, especially as the pace of change and the complexity of life escalate. In this regard, the benefits of the commons are not simply for college and university students, or for those whose profession is teaching (and who explicitly embrace the scholarship of teaching and learning), but for everyone. The chapter includes recommendations aimed at enlarging the commons and fulfilling the promise of the big ideas on which the scholarship of teaching and learning is founded.

Lest we wander too far into abstraction in all of this, we have populated our account with real people and institutions in and through which the scholarship of teaching and learning actually occurs—teachers, students, administrators, courses and curricula, departments and programs, colleges and universities, foundations and associations, conferences and workshops, books, journals, and the Web. In selecting our examples we have privileged one community of scholars in particular. The Carnegie Academy for the Scholarship of Teaching and Learning (or CASTL, as it is called) is not the only community we could have chosen, but we are using it in part because it is large and varied, and in part because it is the one we know best.

The Carnegie Academy for the Scholarship of Teaching (CASTL)

CASTL's higher education program was established in 1997, when Lee S. Shulman became president of the Carnegie Foundation, to give faculty opportunities to better understand and improve college-level teaching and learning in their fields. The program has three parts: an advanced study center for individual scholars studying their teaching and their students' learning, a campus program for colleges and universities wishing to encourage such work among their faculty, and initiatives with scholarly societies seeking to promote pedagogical scholarship in their fields. At the time of this writing, the program has involved 137 CASTL Scholars as fellows at the advanced study center, over two hundred campuses, twenty-some scholarly and professional societies, and an annual colloquium at the national conference of our partner organization, the American Association for Higher Education (AAHE). Numerous publications and other kinds of products have been produced along the way by Carnegie, AAHE, and the program's many participants as well.

Who are the CASTL Scholars and others involved in these activities? Virtually all have held mainstream faculty positions in a wide array of disciplines, in all types of institutions, and at all stages and stations of an academic career; most are from the United States, but the program also invites international participation. They have come to the work with experience in a range of teaching and learning communities—on campus, in their fields, and in the company of others with commitments to particular pedagogical approaches. And they have all engaged in a project—or a series of projects because one often leads to another—addressing important issues in their classrooms, institutions, and fields.

We were able to draw on their projects for examples of the scholarship of teaching and learning because they have documented their work so that others can learn from it and so that they themselves can benefit from colleagues' comments and critique. Of course, we know these scholars through their work in the CASTL program. But because of their commitment to going public, we have also been able to consult their conference presentations, published articles and essays, and experiments with newer modes of documentation, like electronic course portfolios, which can capture better than standard print the complexity of learning in a particular course, at a particular place and time. In addition, we have surveyed the CASTL Scholars to find out more about the place of this work in their institutions, disciplines, and careers (see the appendix at the back of this book), interviewed several in depth for this and other publications (Hutchings, 2000, 2002; Huber, 2004), and have had, in a few cases, the privilege of speaking with their students about the experience of studying with them.

Our involvement with the CASTL program has also given us access to other communities and efforts from which we draw evidence and examples. Over the last decade a number of initiatives have arisen that invoke the same core ideas that animate Carnegie's work: a view of teaching as intellectual work, a commitment to documenting the work of the classroom in ways that are widely accessible and useful, and a focus on faculty roles and rewards as well as on new ideas about student learning. We have drawn on these other efforts—for instance, a five-campus project on the peer review of course portfolios headquartered at the University of Nebraska, a national initiative on the use of multimedia in the teaching of the humanities based at Georgetown University, an NSF-funded Center for the Integration of Research, Teaching and Learning in the sciences, and several developments outside the United States—seeing them as parallel projects, with highly relevant experiences and lessons to offer. We have turned to survey findings by others that place our own in a broader context. And we have (some will perhaps say excessively) grounded our assertions in a wide range of resources from around the world, believing that habits of citation are part of what is most needed to make the otherwise often fugitive work of teaching and learning grist for a commons with broad reach and significant potential to improve practice.

The scholarship of teaching and learning is not a magic bullet that will shoot through higher education and suddenly solve the many challenges to successful student learning today. But it *is* a tool, an attitude, and an evolving set of habits that faculty and institutions can use to strengthen the educational enterprise. The scholarship of teaching and learning taps into faculty strengths and interests and speaks to the imperative in all professions to find ways to learn from the complex circumstances of practice and to "make new sense of the situations of uncertainty or uniqueness" that arise on a daily basis (Schön, 1983, p. 61). Understood broadly, as a set of practices that can be embraced by all faculty, it has, we believe, the power to change the way teaching is undertaken and to make better learners of us all.

Acknowledgments

One of the great pleasures of writing this book has been the generosity of people whose work and thinking have contributed to our own.

Lee Shulman must be mentioned first. As president of The Carnegie Foundation for the Advancement of Teaching since 1997, he has provided a powerful and generative vision for the scholarship of teaching and learning. We are grateful to him not only for the critical intelligence he has brought to the movement and to our thinking about it but also for his creativity, energy, and humanity. Without his involvement and commitment, the scholarship of teaching and learning would surely be a less interesting, less consequential phenomenon than the one we describe in these pages.

Many of our ideas have been influenced and improved by close work with other Carnegie Foundation colleagues—more of them than can, alas, be mentioned here. We are grateful, especially, to Richard Gale, director of the Carnegie Academy for the Scholarship of Teaching and Learning, for the ready supply of fresh ideas and careful feedback; to project manager Marcia Babb, who has been with the program from its early days and whose sense of its history has been an invaluable resource; and to Randy Bass, whose role as consultant and collaborator has helped shape our thinking. Thanks also to Sherry Hecht for endless hours of work on the manuscript, to Megan Gutelius for help in tracking down elusive sources, to Gay Clyburn for assistance in the editing and production of the volume, and to Rebecca Cox, who took the lead in the survey of CASTL Scholars that appears in the appendix and helped shape our conclusions.

One of the central themes of this volume is that the scholarship of teaching and learning brings together and benefits from involvement by many different communities. Among these, none has been more important than the American Association for Higher Education, Carnegie's partner in the CASTL program from 1998 to 2005, and no one at AAHE has been a better colleague than Barbara Cambridge. She has almost single-handedly shepherded along the CASTL Campus Program, and her leadership is responsible for many of the exciting developments we report in this volume.

Most important, we want to thank the scholars whose work provides the examples discussed in this book. Most are faculty who have been active in the CASTL program. But their work, in turn, has helped to involve many additional colleagues on their campuses and in their scholarly and professional societies. And these colleagues too have become participants in an increasingly interconnected network of scholars, who are helping to build the teaching commons. All of these individuals have taken risks by becoming involved in this emergent area of work and then raised the stakes even higher by sharing their experiences, both positive and negative, along the way—and then allowing us to share them further.

We are grateful too to the CASTL Scholars who participated in our survey. Virtually all respondents contributed thoughtful and detailed comments to the open-ended questions, and demonstrated tremendous generosity with their already scarce time and energy. Their willingness to help and their interest in the results are very much appreciated.

We thank too all those who contributed advice and assistance in drafting and revising the questionnaire (Rose Asera, Marcia Babb, Randy Bass, Elizabeth Beaumont, Richard Gale, and Alex McCormick), participating in the pilot (five CASTL Scholars—Hessel Bouma, Lendol Calder, Wendy Ostroff, Caroline Persell, and Deborah Vess), and coordinating the distribution, collection, and organization of the survey (Lindsay Turner).

We have been fortunate in finding colleagues to comment on and critique manuscript versions of this book. Marcia Babb, Randy Bass, Barbara Cambridge, Gay Clyburn, Richard Gale, and Lee Shulman honored our request with close readings and hard questions. A special word of thanks is due to our external reviewers, Barbara Walvoord and two others, whose names we still do not know. Their careful, provocative appraisals and constructive suggestions have been most gratefully taken to heart in our revision. Thanks, too, to our wonderful colleagues at Jossey-Bass for their careful attention to the editorial and production process.

Both the writing of this book and the developments we write about owe a huge debt of gratitude to several organizations that have provided financial support for Carnegie's work on the scholarship of teaching and learning. CASTL was launched in 1998 in partnership with The Pew Charitable Trusts. Subsequently, the work has benefited from Carnegie's collaborations with The William and Flora Hewlett Foundation and the Wabash College Center of Inquiry in the Liberal Arts. Indeed, though we refer in this book to the faculty who have participated in the Carnegie program as CASTL Scholars, they were originally called Pew Fellows, then Carnegie Scholars, and some, in more recent cohorts, are also Center of Inquiry Scholars.

Our interest in the scholarship of teaching and learning goes back quite a number of years, and we have naturally written about it in venues and vehicles previous to this one. With thanks and permission from esteemed coauthors, we have drawn from those previous (and, in one or two cases, future) publications in this book, and have, of course, acknowledged them in the text and references.

The growth of the teaching commons is testimony to the far reach and vibrancy of the scholarship of teaching and learning today. We are grateful, both personally and professionally, to have been involved in this work, and to have had this opportunity to convey our excitement about its promise for higher education.

ABOUT THE AUTHORS

MARY TAYLOR HUBER is a senior scholar at The Carnegie Foundation for the Advancement of Teaching, where she directs the Integrative Learning Project and works closely with the Carnegie Academy for the Scholarship of Teaching and Learning. Since joining the Foundation in 1985, she has written widely on changing cultures of teaching in higher education and is coauthor of the Foundation report, *Scholarship Assessed: Evaluation of the Professoriate* (1997), coeditor of *Disciplinary Styles in the Scholarship of Teaching and Learning: Exploring Common Ground* (2002), and author of *Balancing Acts: The Scholarship of Teaching and Learning in Academic Careers* (2004). A cultural anthropologist, with a doctorate from the University of Pittsburgh, she has also written on colonial societies and is coeditor of *Gendered Missions: Women and Men in Missionary Discourse and Practice* (1999) and *Irony in Action: Anthropology, Practice, and the Moral Imagination* (2001).

PAT HUTCHINGS is vice president of The Carnegie Foundation for the Advancement of Teaching, working closely with a wide range of programs and research initiatives, including the Carnegie Academy for the Scholarship of Teaching and Learning. Hutchings joined the Foundation in February 1998 after serving as a senior staff member at the American Association for Higher Education (AAHE). She has written widely on the investigation and documentation of teaching and learning, the peer collaboration and review of teaching, and the scholarship of teaching and learning. Recent publications, both drawing from Carnegie's work, include *Ethics of Inquiry: Issues in the Scholarship of Teaching and Learning* (2002) and *Opening Lines: Approaches to the Scholarship of Teaching and Learning* (2000). She holds a doctorate in English from the University of Iowa and was chair of the English department at Alverno College from 1978–1987.

The works or acts of merit towards learning are conversant about three objects; the places of learning, the books of learning; and the persons of the learned. For as water, whether it be the dew of heaven, or the springs of the earth, doth scatter and leese itself in the ground, except it be collected into some receptacle, where it may by union comfort and sustain itself; and for that cause the industry of man hath made and framed spring-heads, conduits, cisterns, and polls, which men have accustomed likewise to beautify and adorn with accomplishments of magnificence and state, as well as of use and necessity; so this excellent liquor of knowledge, whether it descend from divine inspiration, or spring from human sense, would soon perish and vanish to oblivion, if it were not preserved in books, traditions, conferences, and places appointed, as universities, colleges, and schools, for the receipt and comforting of the same.

Francis Bacon
The Advancement of Learning (1605)

I

SURVEYING THE SCHOLARSHIP OF TEACHING AND LEARNING

We must change the status of teaching from private to community property.[1]

Related to the public domain is the more general idea of "the commons"—resources that are not divided into individual bits of property but rather are jointly held so that anyone may use them without special permission.[2]

IN THIS BOOK WE OFFER a vision of the scholarship of teaching and learning in higher education that calls for a transformation affecting all teachers. Though employed in different ways and to different degrees, the scholarship of teaching and learning entails basic but important principles that can and should be in every professor's repertoire. It means viewing the work of the classroom as a site for inquiry, asking and answering questions about students' learning in ways that can improve one's own classroom and also advance the larger profession of teaching.

Indeed, we see the scholarship of teaching and learning as part of a wider phenomenon that we call the teaching commons, an emergent conceptual space for exchange and community among faculty, students, administrators, and all others committed to learning as an essential activity of life in contemporary democratic society. Thus we bring a broad view to the topic, and a hopeful one. We see the scholarship of teaching and learning not as a corrective to something that has gone wrong, not as a fix for something broken, but as a set of habits and dispositions for meeting the challenges that we all face as learners and citizens in the twenty-first century.

For some time now, college and university professors have been feeling the once-steady ground of classroom teaching shift beneath their feet. Faced with an increasingly diverse student population, new communication technologies, and changing educational priorities, they are doing their best to respond. Across disciplines, institutions, systems, and countries, educators are asking new questions about what to teach in their courses and programs, how best to engage students in learning that matters, and how to help them put the pieces together to find meaning in their college careers. Moreover, they are sharing the answers to these questions in ways that promise to transform higher education.

Consider Dennis Jacobs, a chemistry professor at the University of Notre Dame, who until 1997 taught in a conscientious but conventional way. Writing about his experience, Jacobs notes that things changed when "I began teaching a large general chemistry course with nearly one thousand students divided into four lecture sections. It was a traditional introductory science course, but for me it became a concern when my office hours for the course were dominated by students who were struggling." Poorly prepared in high school, they were "caught off guard" by exams that required real problem solving. And after getting low marks on one or two exams, they would withdraw from the course (Jacobs, 2000, p. 41). This scene has played out over and over again in introductory science and mathematics at colleges and universities of all kinds (Seymour and Hewitt, 1997). It is a failure that is no longer considered an acceptable, if regrettable, par for the course.

In fact, Dennis Jacobs is one of a growing number of faculty who understand that introductory chemistry is a gateway to a number of majors and that, for many students, dropping out of "101" means dropping any dream of being a scientist, an engineer, a doctor. So, instead of just writing them off as "too dumb" for science (Tobias, 1990), Jacobs put his head to the problem. He consulted the growing body of literature about chemistry and physics education, he got help from Notre Dame's teaching and learning center and its office for institutional research, and he created an alternative learning environment for at-risk students, where lectures are interspersed with opportunities for students to work together on challenging problems, defend their ideas, and articulate their understandings. His array of assessments showed that the alternative approach significantly improved retention and achievement in subsequent courses, and convinced faculty in other science fields at Notre Dame to adopt a similar model. Jacobs has received national recognition for his work, and he has presented it in scholarly forums where other faculty can learn from, engage with, and critique his results.[3]

Stories like those of Dennis Jacobs are increasingly common. Often, though not always, flying the flag of "the scholarship of teaching and learning," faculty members in all fields of undergraduate instruction and in all types of institutions are taking teaching public: documenting what they do, engaging in classroom inquiry, gathering evidence, and building and sharing knowledge to improve practice. This book is about the ways in which these faculty are going about their work as teachers, and how they are helping to build a larger commons through that work.

The Scholarship of Teaching and Learning

Introduced into the vocabulary of higher education by *Scholarship Reconsidered* (Boyer, 1990), the scholarship of teaching and learning gained a hearing less because of its novelty or precision than because it gave teaching a place in a broader vision of scholarship that also included discovery through basic research and efforts to advance the integration and application of knowledge. As a scholarly enterprise, Boyer wrote, "Teaching is . . . a dynamic endeavor involving all the analogies, metaphors, and images that build bridges between the teacher's understanding and the student's learning. Pedagogical procedures must be carefully planned, continuously examined, and relate directly to the subject taught" (pp. 23–24). By focusing on the intellectual demands of teaching in *Scholarship Reconsidered,* and especially in its sequel, *Scholarship Assessed* (Glassick, Huber, and Maeroff, 1997), Boyer and his colleagues attempted to foreground what the scholarship of teaching and learning shares with other kinds of scholarly work (see Rice, 1991).[4]

Meanwhile, a host of related developments gave further momentum and substance to the concept. Scholars of teaching and learning were able to draw on a long-standing literature on teacher knowledge (for example, Shulman, 1987; Grossman, Wilson, and Shulman, 1989), and on more recent research into the character of learning itself (Bransford, Brown, and Cocking, 1999; Marchese, 1997). The assessment movement, and especially the phenomenon of classroom assessment, sharpened higher education's focus on student learning and provided tools for faculty seeking to investigate the impact of their course designs and pedagogies on student learning (Angelo and Cross, 1993; Cross and Steadman, 1996). An interest in course and teaching portfolios and other strategies for the peer review of teaching expanded the audience for teaching to include colleagues as well as students (Edgerton, Hutchings, and Quinlan, 1991;

Centra, 1993; Shulman, 1993; Hutchings, 1996; Seldin, 1997). The 1990s were also a decade that saw the establishment and growth of teaching and learning centers, which, on many campuses, provided programming and support for faculty reflecting on and sharing their teaching practice. More recently, many of these centers have explicitly embraced the agenda and language of the scholarship of teaching and learning, as have many of the scholarly and professional societies.

As the scholarship of teaching and learning has evolved and been enriched by intersections with related initiatives, its boundaries have been subject to debate; indeed, much of the discussion has been about definitions and distinctions. For one thing, it has become clear that there are elements of discovery, integration, and application within the scholarship of teaching and learning, because this work typically involves classroom inquiry, synthesizing ideas from different fields, and the improvement of practice, all at the same time. It is also clear that the scholarship of teaching and learning may look different in different disciplines. To be sure, many pedagogical issues and topics cut across fields. But most faculty members think about teaching and learning inside the framework of their own (and closely related) fields, which is also where many of their best aspirations for students lie. Biologists, historians, and psychologists may all agree that they want to foster deep understanding in their college classrooms, but what they mean by deep understanding is different (Donald, 2002; see also Becher and Trowler, 2001), and so too is the way they are likely to go about the scholarship of teaching and learning (Healey, 2002; Huber, 2000; Huber and Morreale, 2002a; Lueddeke, 2003). Finally, there have been many useful attempts to parse the work into different stages or levels of elaboration (see, for example, Hutchings and Shulman, 1999; Kreber, 2001, 2002, 2003; Kreber and Cranton, 2000; Richlin, 2001, 2003; Trigwell, Martin, Benjamin, and Prosser, 2000; Trigwell, 2004).

In the face of different images of the scholarship of teaching and learning, the two of us have come to embrace a capacious view of the topic, wanting to draw this movement in the broadest possible terms—as a big tent, if you will, under which a wide range of work can thrive. The core of that work includes the kinds of inquiry and investigation that faculty are most likely to undertake when they examine and document teaching and learning in their classrooms in order to improve their practice and make it available to peers. But this work can include (at one end) studies with elaborate research designs and formal execution that go beyond a single classroom, program, or discipline, as well as (at the other end) quite modest efforts to document and reflect on one's teaching and share what one has learned.

Whatever its shape or approach, it is difficult work that tends to run against the grain of academic culture. Faculty today are being asked to do more than ever, with fewer resources, greater accountability, and uncertain rewards. In this climate, calls for a scholarship of teaching and learning can easily be seen as loading even more on weary professorial backs. Done well, however—which means voluntarily and with the right level of support—such work can be empowering for faculty and for their students. Through the scholarship of teaching and learning, faculty can systematically improve the educational environments they create in their own courses and programs and help build the larger commons in ways that support the work of others in their institutions and disciplines seeking to foster the kinds of learning needed today.

The Teaching Commons: What's at Stake

Higher education has long fostered the robust commons created by scientific and scholarly research. This has not been the case with teaching and learning. Until quite recently, serious research on the education of college students was the province of relatively small, disconnected communities of scholars reading and contributing to the newsletters, journals, and conferences where pedagogical issues in their fields were aired. Their work has much to offer, but many college and university faculty were not aware of it. For the large majority, conversations about teaching and learning were local, even fugitive affairs, confined to college and departmental committees and to circles of close friends. No wonder teaching was so often undervalued. As Lee Shulman observed in one of the key texts of the movement to build a scholarship of teaching and learning, teaching will not be fully recognized in the academy until its status changes from "private to community property" (1993, p. 6). Without a functioning commons, it is hard for pedagogical knowledge to circulate, deepen through debate and critique, and inform the kinds of innovation so important to higher education today.

In many arenas—natural resources, the Internet, scientific research—the notion of the commons tends to be invoked to mourn its passing or warn against its loss. For better or worse, history provides many examples of shifts from public to private control, from the enclosure movement in England, in which the landed classes took over open fields traditionally managed by local communities, to the recent trend for business interests to seek greater sway over the use of public resources, such as land, water, the airwaves, the Internet, and the results of federally funded research (Bollier, 2001; Lessig, 1999). As the higher education community glimpsed in the rush to e-learning in the 1990s, the field of teaching and learning is potentially as vulnerable to enclosure as other intellectual and cultural resources (McSherry, 2001). But the more immediate challenge is to strengthen and enlarge the commons that is now taking shape, to make teaching, in the words of one report, "a subject of common engagement within the academy" (Knight Higher Education Collaborative, 2002, p. 1; see also Zemsky and Massy, 2004).

The elements of a teaching commons are developing at a rapid pace. On campuses, a wide array of educational initiatives are converging on issues of teaching and learning, including reforms in graduate education like the Preparing Future Faculty program, the design of opportunities for integrative learning throughout the curriculum, and the introduction and refinement of course management systems and other technology initiatives. Higher education associations and scholarly societies have increased the amount of air and column space they give to educational issues, in part because knowledge practices are changing in many fields. In the humanities, for example, the new media and the access they afford to primary documents in history, literature, and culture have transformed possibilities for undergraduate instruction. And the sciences have enjoyed unprecedented levels of funding for projects in teaching and learning, reflecting changes in national policy that have emphasized recruiting and retaining women and minorities in science fields, as well as raising the level of scientific literacy for science and nonscience majors alike (Seymour, 2002).

Many of these developments and issues have an international dimension. Scholars in the United States are finding lively colleagues in countries like Canada, the United Kingdom, Ireland, Australia, and New Zealand, where there are strong traditions of pedagogical research (see Kreber, 2002). The International Symposium on Improving Student Learning, organized by the Oxford Center for Staff and Learning Development of Oxford-Brookes University in England, has been meeting annually since 1992. City University of London has sponsored an international conference on the scholarship of teaching and learning for several years, and the newly formed International Society for the Scholarship of Teaching and Learning promises to bring even larger and more diverse communities together. Developments in the European Union also appear to be moving in a direction that calls for more systematic attention to undergraduate instruction, and indeed, globalization is pushing similar developments in countries everywhere that are hoping to attract international students or send their own students to study abroad (see, for example, Centre for Higher Education Research & Information, 2004). In short, it is fair to say that the teaching commons is growing in size, diversity, and momentum.

The development and stewardship of this commons matters not only to faculty and students but to all who care about the quality of higher education and its larger social role. What happens in the classroom (and in laboratories, internships, field sites, and the like) is critical to what students actually learn in college and to their future personal, professional, and civic lives. One of higher education's proudest achievements has been to increase access for high school graduates and for adults returning to college in countries around the world. Assuring access remains a continuing challenge, especially in hard economic times. But with globalization raising the bar for productive employment and responsible citizenship, educators everywhere are recognizing that access alone is not enough. As Patti Gumport and Robert Zemsky (2003) argue, today's urgent policy issues must now include "access to what?" (see also National Center for Postsecondary Improvement, 2002).

Certainly, "access to what?" is a question that is turning policymakers' attention to teaching and learning in the United States. Congressional debates on higher education policy focus on how to ensure that college students are receiving a quality education; the National Center for Public Policy in Higher Education is seeking measures of student outcomes for its state-by-state report card; researchers are constructing new measures of undergraduate experience, like the National Survey of Student Engagement; accrediting agencies, like the Western Association of Schools and Colleges or the Accrediting Board for Engineering and Technology, are adding criteria about student learning; and colleges and universities themselves are experimenting with a variety of new assessments and approaches in which students document, reflect on, and connect the different facets of their education.[5]

Pedagogy Moves Center Stage

For most of the history of higher education in the United States, the form and content of the curriculum have been the most common sites for realigning college studies with changes in the larger social and scholarly worlds. What makes today's situation unusual is that pedagogy has finally slipped off the cloak of tradition, and, like other institutions of cultural transmission that are no longer taken for granted, become "controversial, conscious, constructed: a matter of decision, will, and effort" (Bailyn, 1960, p. 48).

This is not to say that pedagogy remained unchanged for over four hundred years. Indeed, there were important shifts, most notably in the mid- to late nineteenth century, when the prescribed curriculum of classical and literary studies was replaced with the elective system in which students could choose among courses in the modern arts and sciences. Debates raged about how to make room for these new fields of knowledge in college study, but without much fanfare classroom teaching changed as well. Laboratories and seminars replaced traditional recitations and disputations, and the old goals of mental training gave way to inquiry and critical thinking as valued habits of mind.[6] Indeed, this new understanding of learning made it possible for educators to see pedagogical virtue in the elective system itself. According to historian Julie Reuben: "Instructors expected students to question established views, learn how to gather and evaluate evidence in favor of theories, and judge for themselves the adequacy of various positions. Electives accorded well with the ideals of open inquiry because they required students to make free choices. . . . [They] encouraged the same habits of mind required by scientific inquiry, and university policies were thus seen to reflect [these] ideals" (1996, p. 67).

In the early twentieth century, colleges and universities continued to accommodate new disciplines, professions, and civic institutions by changing the curriculum to meet new needs. Yet as the subjects of study proliferated, and as the numbers and kinds of students coming to college grew and diversified, educational leaders of that era became concerned. Was there a way to strike a balance between the two basic models of undergraduate study that they had inherited from the past: the one oriented toward community and the authority of tradition, and the other embracing individual choice and the critical spirit of science?[7] Following Harvard's introduction of distribution and specialization requirements in 1910, most colleges and universities settled on some variation of general education for freshmen and sophomores and in-depth study in "the major" for juniors and seniors (Rudolph, 1977). This produced a remarkably flexible arrangement that could accommodate society's need for both a liberally educated citizenry and a workforce prepared for the modern, specialized professions required to manage the new, industrialized economy (see Goldin, 2001).

The very flexibility of this compromise kept colleges and universities open to debate about the content of the curriculum—though seldom how it was taught. What subjects should all college students study? What should be open to choice? How could an institution balance the goals of liberal learning with the logic of disciplinary specialization, especially when general education was channeled into options offered and controlled by different departments? A steady stream of new academic fields and professional studies pushed in the direction of curricular growth and fragmentation, periodically calling forth reformers who pushed back for community and a common curricular core. Writing in the late 1970s, Ernest Boyer and Arthur Levine identified three such revivals centering around World War I, World War II, and again in response to a sense of national crisis following the cultural upheavals of the 1960s and concerns about American economic competitiveness in the world economy (1981).[8]

Other, less heralded innovations accompanied this pulse of public debates about the size and shape of the curriculum. For example, the progressive college movement of the 1920s and 1930s produced experiments, such as those at Sarah Lawrence College, where students designed their own courses of study, received no grades, and contributed labor toward the upkeep of the institution (Kimball, 2003). The "Great Books" curriculum and undergraduate seminars that developed at the University of Chicago in the 1930s and 1940s influenced the design of honors programs around the country. New cluster colleges and interdisciplinary programs encouraging independent study sprang up in the wake of student unrest in the 1960s. And here and there, older traditions of classroom teaching were transformed. Emergent fields like composition and women's studies brought ideas about critical pedagogy into wider view, while innovative attempts to adapt pedagogical ideas from developmental psychology and behavioral psychology (mastery learning, or "the Keller Plan") also flourished for a while.

For much of the twentieth century, however, conversations about teaching and learning in college remained backstage. Certainly, there were influential statements by educational leaders, and important reports, like the Harvard "Red Book" with its vision for the post–World War II liberal arts (Harvard Committee, 1945). Occasionally, too, intellectual leaders like Nobel Prize–winning scientists or presidents of prominent scholarly societies weighed in on educational issues. Dedicated pedagogical researchers worked in shadowy corners of their disciplines and institutions. Faculty attending the annual conferences of their disciplines could take in a few sessions on teaching. And a small number of societies sponsored specialized educational journals, like the American Society for Engineering Education, which began producing a newsletter in 1910, and the Division of Chemical Education of the American Chemical Society, which has published the *Journal of Chemical Education* since 1924.

However, it was only during the explosive era of growth and challenge of the late 1960s that pedagogical issues found regular outlets for dissemination, discussion, and debate in the wider higher education community, many of which remain current today.[9] During this period, there was an intensification of scholarly research on all domains of academic life, pedagogy included. The Carnegie Commission on Higher Education (later, the Carnegie Council on Policy Studies in Higher Education) initiated an extraordinarily influential series of studies in 1969, while the *Chronicle of Higher Education, Change,* and Jossey-Bass all started publishing news, commentary, and books at about the same time. The Department of Education's Fund for the Improvement of Postsecondary Education (FIPSE) began supporting pilot projects on campuses around the country in 1972 (Miller, 2002), and, in the 1980s, the National Science Foundation began to introduce new initiatives to expand, broaden, and improve undergraduate education in science, technology, engineering, and mathematics, engaging not only educational specialists but mainstream faculty as well (Seymour, e-mail to the authors, April 18, 2005; see also Seymour, 2001; Wankat, Felder, Smith, and Oreovicz, 2002).

Amid this ferment, pedagogy—long in the background—began to move forward, if not to the center of the stage. Increasingly, even questions about curriculum and content morphed into concerns about crosscutting dispositions and skills, and faculty began to design courses that would teach both subject matter and the intellectual arts of critical thinking, creativity, and problem solving. Reformers urged campuses to extend general education into the upper years and to redesign the major to serve similar crosscutting intellectual goals. Indeed, as more and more students enrolled in preprofessional degree programs rather than the traditional arts and sciences, educators began to see liberal education itself less as a matter of what subjects are studied than of how they are taught.

As pedagogy moved to the foreground, it was perhaps inevitable that long-established teaching practices would be questioned from outside colleges and universities as well as from within. Large lecture classes with little opportunity for students to interact with the professor became a popular emblem for whatever people deemed wrong with higher education. The nation's research universities were criticized for not paying sufficient attention to the education of undergraduates, delegating much introductory teaching to poorly supported graduate students or short-term instructors, and focusing recognition and reward on faculty research at the expense of teaching. Finally, concerned with rapidly rising tuition, critics also began questioning the meaning of the baccalaureate degree, asking institutions to take responsibility for what undergraduate students actually learned during their college years. How well, people wanted to know, were colleges preparing students for the new global economy and for life in the uncharted waters of the post–cold war years? Could they do better?[10]

The College Classroom on Shifting Ground

If it were possible to swoop down over the nation's colleges and universities and peer into the work of teaching and learning today, it would be clear, very quickly, how dramatically in the last two to three decades the college classroom has changed. These changes are spurring the growth of the commons because they provoke educators to ask questions about teaching and learning that cannot be answered easily through conventional wisdom and resources alone.

Many changes are well known. For starters, the traditional student entering college full-time right after high school, supported by parents or working only part-time, is now "the exception rather than the rule. In 1999–2000, just 27 percent of undergraduates met all of these criteria" (Choy, 2002, p. 1). More than 40 percent of undergraduates in 1999–2000 were older than twenty-four years, more than a quarter were thirty or older, and nearly half of undergraduates attended college part-time. Today, many students have families and jobs that necessarily take precedence over schoolwork, so that after class they rush back to work or go home to family responsibilities. Classrooms are increasingly populated with men and women who are the first in their families to attend college, and who are sometimes unfamiliar with the routines and expectations of academic life. Indeed, in 1999–2000, 37 percent of undergraduates were first-generation college goers. Individuals identified as ethnic or racial minority accounted for 32 percent of all undergraduates in higher education in 1999–2000, up from 26 percent in 1995, and 17 percent in 1976 (Horn, Peter, Rooney, and Malizio, 2002).

The subjects that students study have also changed. Preprofessional programs continue to grow, and are being recast with links to the liberal arts. Disciplines are changing. The canon of works studied in college has become multicultural, including books by women, authors from ethnic and racial minority groups, and writers and scholars from around the world. Stanford University English professor Andrea Lunsford invites us, for instance, to "look around [English where] . . . you will find a very broad definition of 'literature' and of reading, a definition that clearly includes film, video, multimedia and hypertext, and discourses not traditionally thought of as 'literature' (such as Deaf and Spoken Word poetry, cookbooks, tombstone inscriptions) right alongside studies of canonical writers and their print texts" (Lunsford, 2006).

Indeed, the contours of most disciplines have shifted significantly. For example, Hyman Bass, past president of the American Mathematical Society, notes that mathematics has become "much more out in the world than it was even a quarter century ago. There are more directions of exploration within mathematics, with a greater diversity of tools and methods; there are substantial interdisciplinary interventions of mathematics in a variety of fields; the utility of mathematics for many problems of science and society is increasingly evident; and mathematics has a growing presence in administrative and policy environments, both in universities and at the national level" (Bass, 2006).

And for many students and faculty much of the most exciting work today occurs in the shifting boundaries between fields, be it in biochemistry, American studies, or more ad hoc conjunctions. In short, there is far less agreement now about what is most important to teach and to learn.

Along with changes in students and content come changes in pedagogy. One of the myths that dogs discussions of higher education is that classroom approaches are frozen in time. As we have argued, however, that view fails to account for shifts that have occurred historically and that are accelerating today. According to the Higher Education Research Institute Faculty Survey, the proportion of faculty who report "extensive lecturing" has gone from 55.7 in 1989–90, to 48.5 in 1995–96, to 46.9 in 2001–02 (Astin, Korn, and Dey, 1991; Sax, Astin, Arredondo, and Korn, 1996; Lindholm, Astin, Sax, and Korn, 2002). The wonderful title of Donald Finkel's *Teaching with Your Mouth Shut* (2000) is telling in this regard, representing a view of teaching based more on engaging students, listening to them, and involving them in their own learning. The literature today documents a growing commitment to new (or newly discovered) pedagogies, including problem-based learning, community-based learning, service learning, and undergraduate research. And of course, technology continues to generate new discussions, experiments, and tools for teaching and learning.

Different pedagogies entail different kinds of assignments and assessments aimed at different purposes and outcomes. Even a cursory scan of goals listed in contemporary course syllabi reveals a focus on cross-cutting abilities and dispositions that was not so common in the past. Tasks required of students have changed accordingly. In addition to the traditional, all-but-ubiquitous research paper, or instead of it, students today may be asked to write for real audiences in the community; individual intellectual work, the long-standing coin of the academic realm, is now complemented by a strong dose of group work and collaborative projects. Students may find that part of their grade depends on collaboration with others in developing a presentation for their fellow students, or a multimedia Web site that can be seen by others around the world. They may find guidelines in the syllabus for assignments that take them outside the classroom to work in a service learning setting in the community.[11]

It is hardly necessary to mention recent transformations in the material culture of teaching. Participation in distance education is rising among undergraduates, as well as among graduate and professional-degree students. In many fields, faculty and students are using electronic archives, technical computing software, computer-aided design, simulation systems, and the like. The use of e-mail and the Web is everywhere in academe. And beyond the pioneers and early adopters, mainstream faculty are rethinking classroom practice with these new tools in mind. How does one manage and make good use of e-mail communication with students? How does one manage and make good use of course-specific Web sites, with the opportunities afforded for collaborative learning by widely adopted "learning systems" such as Blackboard and WebCT? What do the new technologies mean for assignments and assessment? How are new media changing the nature of expert practice in one's field? Do these changes in how mathematicians, scientists, social scientists, humanists, or management professionals conduct their work alter what and how students should learn about these fields and what and how their teachers should teach? (Huber, 2004; see also Ayers, 2004; Batson and Bass, 1996; Brown, 2000; Laurillard, 2002.)

All of these changes—in students, content, methods, assessment, and technology—invite pedagogical inquiry. Sometimes educators' questions lead them to an electronic discussion list, down the hall to the office of a colleague, to technical support staff, or to a campus center for teaching and learning. Increasingly, the path also leads to a workshop or conference session, and to books, articles, or online resources in their own or a neighboring field. For those who keep asking pedagogical questions, like Dennis Jacobs, the chemist at Notre Dame, this process of inquiry can lead even further, to making their own contributions to the growing body of knowledge about teaching and learning. This is what the teaching commons is all about. Through the combined efforts of educators across the country—and around the world—college teaching is beginning to look more like other professional fields, with a literature and communities that study and advance critical aspects of practice.

Our argument, then, is that the scholarship of teaching and learning is an imperative for higher education today, not a choice. Embracing it means taking ownership of the challenges posed by shifting circumstances, which, though challenging, are also, properly defined, intellectually engaging, generative, and potentially consequential. Scholars of teaching and learning understand classroom difficulties as problems and puzzles to be systematically explored and addressed in ways that contribute to a growing teaching commons. To move teaching from "private to community property," to build a robust commons on a large scale, will require all the intelligence, commitment, and imagination that the academic community can bring to bear. But the movement to do so is, we believe, one of the most hopeful signs that the academy will be able to fulfill its changing teaching mission in the years to come.

NOTES

1. This epigraph is from Lee S. Shulman's "Teaching as Community Property: Putting an End to Pedagogical Solitude" (1993), one of the foundational essays for the scholarship of teaching and learning. The reason teaching is not more valued in the academy, Shulman argues, is not because campuses do not care about it but "because the way we treat teaching removes it from the community of scholars" (p. 6). Thus, he calls for teaching's reconnection to the disciplinary and professional communities in which faculty pursue their scholarly work—a change that would require faculty to document their pedagogical work and make it available to their peers.
2. This epigraph is from the Creative Commons Web site (http://creativecommons.org). As reporter Andrea Foster explains in the *Chronicle of Higher Education* (2004), "Creative Commons is a group that developed an alternative copyright system to make literature, music, films, and scholarship freely available to the public. Now it plans to do the same for scientific and technological research . . . through an alternative licensing scheme."
3. Jacobs's approach to introductory chemistry has been adopted in physics and engineering at Notre Dame, and he is now exploring ways to include service learning in undergraduate chemistry. For information about his scholarship of teaching and learning, see his Web site: http://www.nd.edu/~djacobs/educ.html. His alternate approach to teaching general chemistry is further documented in an electronic portfolio: see Jacobs, 2001.
4. We draw in this section on Huber, Hutchings, and Shulman (2005).
5. Although there is now wide agreement that institutions of higher education should be accountable to the public for student outcomes, there is little agreement about which outcomes colleges and universities should—or could—account for. See, for example, the opinions of eight higher education leaders in "How Can Colleges Prove They're Doing Their Jobs?" in

the *Chronicle of Higher Education* (2004). As the introduction to that article notes, lack of agreement on this issue may have contributed to the failure of Congress to reauthorize the Higher Education Act in 2004. The National Center for Public Policy in Higher Education (2004) has given all states an incomplete on "learning" in its biennial report *Measuring Up,* which grades the states on their performance in higher education (see http://measuringup.highereducation.org/qa.cfm). Information about the accreditation agencies' efforts to encourage institutions and programs to monitor learning outcomes is available through their Web sites, and the National Survey of Student Engagement is described at http://www.indiana.edu/~nsse/. See Cambridge 2001 for information about the National Coalition for Electronic Portfolio Research.

6. Historian Julie Reuben writes that it was uncommon for colleges to have lab equipment before the Civil War, but by the 1880s scientists were pointing to the desirability of teaching science not through recitation, where students learned the results of science, but through laboratories, where students could learn how to think scientifically for themselves (1996). "In the new social sciences," Reuben adds, "instructors used the seminar as the counterpart to laboratory studies in the natural sciences" (p. 66). Of course, new approaches did not entirely replace old ones. For example, at Stanford University during the 1890s and early 1900s: "Lectures, recitations, weekly quizzes, and major exams were familiar fare for students . . . and the introduction of laboratories in the sciences and seminars in history and other disciplines broadened the teaching repertoires that professors used in their courses" (Cuban, 1999, p.18).
7. This is a distinction that we take from Fenstermacher (2003), who in turn cites Bruce Kimball's discussion of two complementary but sometimes conflicting emphases in liberal education (1986).
8. Indeed, there is interest in general education (however conceived) as a way of strengthening democracy and civic well-being in Europe and Asia as well as at home (Association of American Colleges and Universities, 2002; Kimball, 2003; Orrill, 1997; Rothblatt, 2003).
9. According to the United States Bureau of the Census (1975) the number of students grew from 2.3 million in 1950 (or 14.2 percent of the eighteen- to twenty-four-year-old population) to 7.9 million in 1970 (or 32.1 percent of the eighteen- to twenty-four-year-old population). The number of institutions and faculty also dramatically increased. In 1950, there were about 1,823 colleges and universities with 190,000 faculty members; in 1970, the numbers were 2,525 institutions with 532,000 faculty (Metzger, 1987, cited in Rosovsky and Hartley, 2002).

10. One of the most influential reports of this kind was *Reinventing Undergraduate Education: A Blueprint for America's Research Universities,* published in 1998 by the Boyer Commission on Educating Undergraduates in the Research University. A series of events and publications organized by the Reinvention Center at Stony Brook have helped sustain interest and encourage innovation in undergraduate education, especially at doctoral and research universities (http://www.sunysb.edu/Reinventioncenter).
11. The new senior assignments at Southern Illinois University-Edwardsville (SIUE) provide an interesting example. Each department designs an assignment that seniors must pass to graduate—it cannot be an examination but instead must be a task for which students demonstrate "in practice an application of what they have learned over their entire undergraduate career" (Association of American Colleges and Universities, 2004, p. 2). The actual kinds of senior assignments required in each department vary—in 2002, for example, anthropology's was a written paper with an oral "conference" presentation, biology's was lab, field, or library research presented in a scientific talk or scientific poster format with oral defense, and theater and dance required a written presentation with an oral defense of a project, or choreography (see SIUE's Web site: http://www.siue.edu/~deder/assess/taba02.html).

2

DEFINING FEATURES

Thinking about teaching begins where all intellectual inquiry begins, with questions about what is going on and how to explain, support, and replicate answers that satisfy us.[1]

HOW EXACTLY TO DEFINE the scholarship of teaching and learning has been the subject of much debate. Like other emergent fields of endeavor (think of biochemistry and women's studies in their formative years—or even snowboarding), the scholarship of teaching and learning does not come cut from whole cloth but builds on existing traditions and lines of work, some of them long-standing. Decades of work by faculty whose research has focused on the pedagogy of their field clearly feeds into today's scholarship of teaching and learning. The assessment movement, too, especially that aspect of assessment that focuses directly on the classroom, is an older cousin. Many campuses have centers for teaching and learning that have promoted scholarly work to improve instruction. And scholars of teaching and learning in higher education owe a debt to the K–12 teacher-research movement and to other disciplines and fields that have developed the methods and paradigms for action research.[2]

If the scholarship of teaching and learning is a phenomenon at the intersection of older lines of work, it is also a movement with new dimensions, new angles, new ambitions. Practices and insights borrowed from various traditions and communities are being adopted by a different and wider group of educators, and, as a consequence, adapted to new purposes and opportunities. Like other new areas of work, this one is a moving target,[3] still taking shape as a larger community of practice forms around it, and as conventions and standards develop around emerging interests and needs.

In this chapter, then, we propose a definition that reflects an evolving set of ideas and practices that can and should shape the work of all faculty as they bring their habits, methods, and commitments as scholars to their work as teachers—and to their students' learning. We do so by looking first at the need for the scholarship of teaching and learning, then at four features that define it, and finally at what it promises for the teaching commons.

Needs and Reasons

One of the best ways to understand the scholarship of teaching and learning is by looking at the need that prompts it. In a nutshell, that need is to capture the work of teaching and learning in ways that can be built upon—to *stop losing* "the intellectual work that is regularly being done," as Dan Bernstein has written, by creating "a community of teachers whose decisions about how to teach will be informed by the collective effectiveness of the work" (2001, pp. 228–229). To put it a bit differently, the problem the scholarship of teaching and learning aims to address is that teaching has, traditionally, had so few ways to improve itself.

As a profession, teaching has long been vexed by perceptions that make its advancement difficult. It's easy: anyone "off the street" can do it. It's magic: not something you learn to do but a gift you are born with. It's technique and tricks, not intellectually substantive. Carrying such baggage, teaching has developed few of the mechanisms that make improvement possible over time. *Individual* faculty work hard at their classroom craft, but the larger, collective enterprise of teaching does not move forward because the work of improvement is so often done in isolation, in the school of hard knocks, one might say, and by the seat of the pants. In contrast, the scholarship of teaching and learning offers the prospect of work in which teachers—to use Sir Isaac Newton's famous image—"stand on the shoulders of giants."[4]

Lee Shulman has written extensively about the need for this shift of perspective. It was as a newly minted faculty member, he recalls, that he felt the first sharp pangs of "pedagogical solitude," the fact that teaching, which might seem to be the most social of work, done in community with others, is much less public than research (1993, p. 6). In fact, teaching is private work for many faculty, taking place behind doors that are both metaphorically and physically closed. Not surprisingly, then, there are few habits or conventions for exploring what teachers do and how it affects their students, and for sharing what they do and know with colleagues who might benefit from it. "Unlike fields such as architecture (which preserves its creations in both plans and edifices), law (which builds a case literature of opinions and interpretations), medicine (with its records and case studies), and even unlike chess, bridge, or ballet (with their traditions of preserving both memorable games and choreographed performances through inventive forms of notation and recording), teaching is conducted without an audience of peers. It is devoid of a history of practice" (Shulman, 1987, pp. 11–12).

Moving teaching from a mostly private enterprise, where what teachers know and do disappears "like dry ice," as Shulman has written, to teaching as "community property," which is documented, shared, and built upon, is a central theme of the scholarship of teaching and learning (1993, p. 7). Such publicness is, after all, part of what is implied when something is called scholarship. One may think brilliant thoughts in the shower, or, for that matter, come to fascinating conclusions in the lab, but, unless new insights are captured in ways that can be shared with others, they are not properly called scholarship. This is not to say that everything that happens in the classroom needs to be made public. Just as not everything that is learned in the library or lab is shared, faculty must be able to make choices about what to document and when to share the work of teaching (see Hutchings, 1996). The confidentiality of student work—an important source of evidence in the scholarship of teaching and learning—must be protected, as well.[5] Faculty and students alike need a safe place to try out new ideas and to bring them to fruition. But that is the point: the fruits are too seldom brought to market. Ongoing improvement will only be possible when the intellectual work of teaching and learning is captured and represented in ways that others can build on.

The need for this shift toward publicness is greater now than ever, for two reasons. First, as described in the previous chapter, the classroom is shifting ground for many faculty today. Growing numbers of students are not prepared for college work. The disciplines are in transition. New technologies, and a whole host of new or newly discovered classroom approaches, bring exciting possibilities but also novel challenges. And ironically perhaps, the more that is known about the social and psychological processes of learning and the science of the brain, the more daunting the work of teaching may feel. Indeed, as our travels have taken us from campus to campus and brought us into conversation with teachers from diverse fields and institutions, we have been struck by a growing sense, perhaps especially among veteran teachers, that what used to work, pedagogically speaking, may not get the job done for today's students. As one former teacher of literature put it, "While I may have been an excellent teacher of British literature twenty years ago, I might not be in today's classroom. I might, but I don't know for certain" (Rhem, 2003, p. 3). The scholarship of teaching and learning is needed today because teaching now is harder than it used to be.

It is also needed because so much interesting pedagogical innovation is being prompted by the challenges of today's educational realities. As University of Pittsburgh English professor Mariolina Salvatori has written (she is referring to her students' learning but the point applies more generally), "moments of difficulty often contain the seeds of understanding" (2000, p. 81), and our work with the scholarship of teaching and learning has persuaded us that the difficulty of teaching is also a spur to real creativity for many faculty and campuses. In short, this is a time of incredible pedagogical ferment and invention, and higher education cannot afford *not* to learn from the innovations and experiments going on in today's classrooms.

Four Defining Features

What, then, does the scholarship of teaching and learning look like? What do faculty who embrace this work actually *do*?

One way to answer this question is to return to the example of Dennis Jacobs, the chemist at Notre Dame whose story introduces the previous chapter. Jacobs looked hard at his students' difficulties in introductory chemistry and saw questions and problems he needed to understand more deeply. He designed a variety of strategies for doing that, including a large-scale study tracking students through subsequent courses but also "up-close" qualitative work through videotaping small groups. As he did this work, and as new insights and evidence emerged, he brought his work to bear on the teaching of the course, applying his new ideas, trying them out, refining approaches as he came to understand them better. As the work progressed he shared what he was learning with colleagues, first in his own setting at Notre Dame but also beyond, for instance at a special forum of the American Chemical Society. His work draws on previous efforts by others, and it is now available for others to build on in turn. Indeed, the work has come full circle—as research generally does—bringing Jacobs to a next set of questions and problems to address.[6]

Certainly not every project in the scholarship of teaching and learning proceeds just as Dennis Jacobs's has. Nevertheless his work is a useful window into four core practices that make up the scholarship of teaching and learning: framing questions, gathering and exploring evidence, trying out and refining new insights in the classroom, and going public with what is learned in ways that others can build on. These practices provide an operational definition of the scholarship of teaching and learning, and we will take them one at a time—though recognizing that the work does not necessarily proceed in a step-by-step, linear way.

Questioning

In our work with scholars of teaching and learning, we have identified a variety of motivations that bring faculty to this work: they may be seeking colleagues who share their interests in pedagogy, they may be looking for ways to bring greater recognition and reward to their work as teachers, they may see themselves as reformers connecting with a national movement they believe has the potential to change higher education. But, as we learned through our recent survey of CASTL Scholars, the single most powerful motivation for becoming involved (identified by 97 percent as somewhat or very important) was having "questions about my students' learning that I wanted to explore" (Cox, Huber, and Hutchings, 2004; see Table 2.1). Indeed, finding and framing questions about student learning is the germ, the catalyst, the first step in the scholarship of teaching and learning.

Frequently the work begins with questions about whether a new classroom strategy or curricular model will promote certain kinds of learning better than a more traditional method. Not surprisingly, such "what works" questions often lead to others that are more open-ended, aimed at uncovering and more deeply understanding "what happens" under particular pedagogical conditions—the use of a simulation to teach about labor law (Corrada, 2001a, 2001b), for instance, or a new model for teaching abnormal psychology that focuses on resilience rather than pathologies (Duffy, 2000). Other questions have a more conceptual and theoretical bent, aiming to articulate new ways *to think about* learning and teaching, which in turn suggest additional questions.[7] In our next chapter we will look at several examples of the scholarship of teaching and learning that take a conceptual turn.

Whatever the thrust and focus of the question, it is, we have seen, the complex, "transactional relation" between teaching and learning that catalyzes this scholarship (Bernstein, 1998, p. 77). As one faculty member writes, the reason to get involved in the scholarship of teaching is not because it is the newest fad or because promotion and tenure guidelines include it but because there is "something you really care about, something you're really interested in learning about" (Cerbin, 2000, p. 19). Serious work on teaching begins, that is, where all scholarship begins, with curiosity and an urge to understand more clearly what is happening and why.

Table 2.1. Reasons for Involvement in the Scholarship of Teaching and Learning

	Percent of Respondents		
	Not Important	Somewhat Important	Very Important
I had questions about my students' learning that I wanted to explore.	3	16	81
I wanted to expand the range of scholarly work in which I am involved.	26	35	39
I wanted to connect my interests in teaching and learning to a recognized body of research.	9	42	50
I wanted to participate in the movement to bring greater recognition and reward to the scholarly work of teaching.	10.5	34.5	54
I wanted to find new colleagues with whom to pursue my interests in teaching and learning.	6	42	52
I was urged to become involved by colleagues who knew about the scholarship of teaching and learning.	48	25.5	26.5

Source: *Cox, Huber, and Hutchings, CASTL Scholars Survey, 2004.*

And the "what" in question—the focus of inquiry and investigation—is student learning.

Faculty's questions about their students' experience as learners may focus on individual courses, on clusters of courses, or on whole programs; they may focus on particular kinds of learning (say, in interdisciplinary settings), or on particular groups of students (women in engineering or students for whom English is a second language). Some questions can be pursued by individual faculty investigating their own classrooms; others require teams of faculty looking across settings and working together to share data and deliberate about their conclusions—sometimes with support from an office of institutional research or assessment, or a center for teaching excellence.

For most faculty the most compelling and urgent questions emerge directly from their own practice. Take, for example, the burgeoning interest in technology. As faculty today employ new digital archives, as they require students to collaborate online, as they move whole courses onto the Web, they encounter (and sometimes are asked by colleagues or administrators) questions about the relative effectiveness of these approaches—especially because technology can entail significant investments of time and money. In this sense, technology is the camel's nose under the teaching tent: it is a small step from questions about the impact of Web-based teaching to questions about other instructional approaches and curricular innovations. Questions about the use of online class discussion in learning communities, for instance, may generate questions about the character of discussion more generally, or about the impact of linked courses on students' ability to integrate their learning across contexts.

To say that student learning raises stimulating questions is not, perhaps, new or startling. But it is worth remembering that teaching is not, for most academics, an arena in which they have developed (or received training to inculcate) habits and skills of inquiry.[8] Georgetown University professor Randy Bass notes the revealing contrast between teaching and research in this regard:

> One telling measure of how differently teaching is regarded from traditional scholarship or research within the academy is what a difference it makes to have a "problem" in one versus the other. In scholarship and research, having a "problem" is at the heart of the investigative process; it is the compound of the generative questions around which all creative and productive activity revolves. But in one's teaching, a "problem" is something you don't want to have, and if you have one, you probably want to fix it. Asking a colleague about a problem in his or her research is an invitation; asking about a problem in one's teaching would probably seem like an accusation. [1999b, p. 1]

Thinking of teaching as a source of interesting, consequential, intellectual problems and questions is a first, defining step in the scholarship of teaching and learning.

Gathering and Exploring Evidence

But asking questions is not enough. As faculty begin to think of teaching as a source of challenging intellectual questions, a second imperative emerges: to devise ways to explore those questions and shed light on them. The scholarship of teaching and learning is not simply a casual interlude of mulling and reflection. Though it may be of limited scope and scale, and therefore modest in one sense, it entails systematic, disciplined inquiry, and requires hard thinking about how to gather and analyze evidence. This process of exploration is, then, the second aspect of our definition.

Looking across the projects undertaken by CASTL Scholars over the past several years, we are struck by the rich array of possibilities that has emerged for gathering and analyzing evidence: course portfolios, the collection and systematic review of student work (sometimes by secondary readers, sometimes with newly devised rubrics that capture aspects of learning that were previously hard to discern), videotape, focus groups, ethnographic interviews, classroom observation, large-scale longitudinal tracking, questionnaires, surveys, and more. This methodological pluralism makes sense. Teaching and learning are complex processes, and no single source or type of evidence can provide a sufficient window into the difficult questions raised by student learning. Sometimes what is needed are data about groups of students, sometimes a "drill down" into the work of a single learner; sometimes numbers speak most clearly, sometimes more qualitative evidence, and often a combination of "counting and recounting" (Shulman, 2004a, p. 165). As in any research, the challenge is to employ the right set of methods and the best sources of evidence to explore the question in ways that will be credible and significant.

But of course, *credible* and *significant* are not adjectives about which everyone agrees. Indeed, it is around issues of method and evidence that disciplinary differences in the scholarship of teaching and learning often surface in ways that are both contested and fruitful. An anecdote from the CASTL program makes the point: A group of faculty from a mix of disciplines was discussing what kinds of work would qualify as scholarship of teaching and learning. How about an in-depth examination of the learning of one student over time? one person proposed. Although some members of the group concurred that such an approach might yield important insights about how learners engage with course material, a sociologist in the group (a past editor of the journal *Teaching Sociology*) objected strenuously. "An *n* of one!" he exclaimed. "That would never count as scholarship in my field" (see Huber, 2000).

He is not alone in this view, of course; many social scientists want to see data that meet their tests for sample size and generalizability, and faculty from the natural sciences and math often share this view. "Scientists are scientists and they know that the data do not lie," reported one scholar from chemistry (Huber, 2000, p. 25). But for scholars in the humanities, *data* (a word they are unlikely even to use) usually means close reading and analysis, not numbers. The experience of a historian contrasts with the comment by the sociologist. T. Mills Kelly began his scholarship of teaching and learning project by looking at the research literature on teaching and technology (his questions were about the impact of his "hybrid" course on students' understanding of world history) where he found himself face-to-face with "a methodology that I knew nothing about—a new language, a use of control groups, a scientific approach." It was not familiar or comfortable ground: "I'm not an educational researcher by training," he reminded us. "I'm an historian." Accordingly, he developed a course portfolio that allowed him to create a kind of history of the course, a genre he was more comfortable with and one that his colleagues in the field found familiar as well (2000, p. 55).

The point is not that the historian (or the sociologist) was right (or wrong) but that different disciplines bring different rules and assumptions about what constitutes credible evidence, and what kinds of methods yield "scholarly" results. Differences of opinion about these matters may make it hard for work to be valued across disciplinary borders. At the same time, it is clear that disciplines can borrow and learn from one another in matters methodological. Certainly this is true in more familiar kinds of research, where, for instance, one can find computer-based content analysis in literary studies and mathematical modeling in the work of historians. Similarly in the scholarship of teaching and learning, borrowing methods from other fields may enrich the process and make lessons learned from the work both deeper and more broadly significant. Thus, in the Carnegie program we have seen microbiologists using discourse analysis (Elmendorf, 2004) and American studies professors using focus group interviews (Linkon, 2000). The important thing is that the method and the question match. Whatever its form, systematic inquiry is central to the scholarship of teaching and learning.

Trying Out and Refining New Insights

Complicating the inquiry process is the fact that the scholarship of teaching and learning occurs in the highly dynamic environment of the classroom (or other learning context). For some faculty, this reality presents a challenge and even a frustration, placing the work in what Donald Schön calls "the swampy lowlands" of scholarship (as opposed to the "high, hard ground") where "problems are messy and confusing and incapable of technical solution" (1995, p. 28).[9] For example, William Cerbin, a psychologist, found himself unable to do the kind of design experiment that he believed his colleagues in psychology would find most credible: "In reality, I was teaching this class as I was experimenting with it and studying it, and under those conditions you sometimes have to change the script as you go because your best judgment tells you that a change would be an improvement for the students. But as a result, I didn't have control, in terms of introducing a certain kind of situation, controlling the variables, and then analyzing student performance" (2000, p. 16). But if this confounding of inquiry and intervention, research and practice, sometimes feels like a limitation, it is also a source of great appeal for many faculty. Those who become involved in systematic investigation of their classrooms almost universally report that the work leads to important changes. Thus, this process of trying out and refining new insights is the third of our four defining features of the scholarship of teaching and learning.

Among CASTL Scholars, for instance, 81 percent agree or strongly agree that the quality of their students' learning has been improved by their work as scholars of teaching and learning. Sixty-nine percent agree or strongly agree that "more of my students achieve high standards of work since I became involved in the scholarship of teaching and learning" (Cox, Huber, and Hutchings, 2004; see Table 2.2). Many also report that their questions about student learning led them to develop more demanding modes of assessment (see, for example, Bernstein, 2000, or Flannery, 2001a).

Sometimes trying out one's findings in practice is more a matter of changed expectations and ambitions than of implementing any particular innovation. Consider this statement from a faculty member in music who became deeply involved in the scholarship of teaching and learning: "[This work] has deeply and permanently changed the way I look at my teaching and my students' learning. The upside is that this has made that aspect of my career exciting. The downside is that I am never, ever satisfied. Once I was rather pleased and even a bit smug about my success as a teacher. Now I see how far I still need to go to truly make a difference in my students' learning, and it feels somewhat overwhelming" (Barkley, Response to CASTL Scholars Survey, 2004).

The point here is that the scholarship of teaching and learning brings with it an expectation that results will not be held at arm's length but rather tried out and used for improvement. As Schön's swamp metaphor suggests, such work is cousin to a wider universe of scholarship that has its center in professional practice and its perennial ambiguities. In short, the scholarship of teaching and learning is often messy rather than neatly linear, engaged rather than disinterested, and highly personal in its impact.

Table 2.2. Consequences of Involvement in the Scholarship of Teaching and Learning

Statement of Consequence	Percent of Respondents: Strongly Disagree	Disagree	Agree	Strongly Agree
I have changed the design of my courses since becoming involved in the scholarship of teaching and learning.	0	6	35	58
I have changed the kinds of assessments I use in my courses as a result of my participation in the scholarship of teaching and learning.	0	8	40	52
My expectations for my students' learning have changed since participating in the scholarship of teaching and learning.	0	8	32	60
I have documented improvements in my students' learning since becoming involved in the scholarship of teaching and learning.	1	15	52	29
More of my students achieve high standards of work since I became involved in the scholarship of teaching and learning.	1	20	49	20

Source: *Cox, Huber, and Hutchings, CASTL Scholars Survey, 2004.*

Going Public

The scholarship of teaching and learning is about more than individual improvement and development—it is about producing knowledge that is available for others to use and build on. This, it should be said, is an ambitious goal, and one that distinguishes the scholarship of teaching and learning from many other approaches to classroom improvement.

For one thing, the scholarship of teaching and learning is not really finished until it has been captured in ways that others can see and examine. Toward this end, scholars of teaching and learning are inventing new genres, forms, and outlets for sharing their work. In addition to traditional journal articles and books, one sees, for instance, the emergence of course portfolios that trace the unfolding of teaching and learning from conception to outcomes (Hutchings, 1998). Many of these portfolios are now electronic, and multimedia technologies have become a powerful resource for revealing not only the final results of a scholarly investigation into teaching and learning but the particular setting, students, and pedagogy. Documentation that preserves these rich details makes it possible for others to ask the all-important question: "Is this work relevant to me and my circumstances?" (Shulman, 2002a, p. vi).

Because its purpose is not only to build new knowledge but to improve practice, the scholarship of teaching and learning lends itself to forms of representation and exchange that are more about engagement than dissemination. The workshop, for instance, has become a staple of campus-based faculty development and of conferences both discipline-based and cross-disciplinary. Or consider the teaching circle, the pedagogical colloquium, the assessment seminar, and the online listserv (like H-Teach, sponsored by the H-NET Humanities and Social Sciences On-Line initiative).[10] These forms of documentation and exchange become a seedbed for new ideas in very much the ways we take for granted in more traditional areas of research scholarship. Indeed, the leader of one national initiative on the scholarship of teaching and learning observes that the faculty he has worked with only fully understand the significance of their own questions and data when they start trying to explain them to others (Randy Bass, e-mail to the authors, November 27, 2004). Going public is not simply a final step in the process—a *t* to be crossed or an *i* to be dotted; instead, it creates new lenses and angles on the entire process and the significance of the work.

As in traditional scholarship, going public also presumes an audience, a community of scholars who will engage with what is captured, documented, and shared. This means thinking in advance about how it will be captured—the genre question, if you will—but also about the most relevant audiences for the work, the communities one seeks to influence, the conversation one seeks to enter and connect with. Many scholars of teaching and learning are interested in engaging colleagues who are close to home—fellow department members, for instance, who teach the same (or similar) students and whose own courses may be enriched by the work. Widening the circle, audiences may also include colleagues from other departments. Campus-based groups are particularly important for asking questions about the local curriculum or innovations aimed at outcomes the campus especially values. But communities need not always be face-to-face. There are larger, more diffuse colleague groups that connect online, read the same journals, and follow the same literature. Some of these focus on a particular pedagogy, like learning communities or service learning. Others are disciplinary. Whether discipline-based or more multidisciplinary, whether close to home or far-ranging, building an audience for this work is an essential component of the scholarship of teaching and learning.

As noted earlier in this chapter, the four elements of the scholarship of teaching and learning need not, and often *do* not, march along in linear fashion. Although it is true that the entry point is often the framing of a question or problem for investigation, the work may also grow from an encounter with the efforts of others at a conference session or in published research, which, in turn, invites a rethinking of evidence that is already at hand (like the stack of student exams sitting on the desk). Or it may be that in testing out a new practice in class, the need to gather more data about students and their learning becomes evident. One of the telling moments in the CASTL summer residency comes when scholars announce, at the end of their fellowship year, after gathering lots of data and going public in all kinds of venues, that they have finally figured out what their project was *really* about. Indeed, like other complex intellectual endeavors (think of writing, for example) the scholarship of teaching and learning is an iterative, "looping" kind of work. And the fact that its four elements occur in all kinds of permutations and rhythms makes it an easier fit with the variable rhythms of faculty life itself.

Moreover, not everyone who ventures into these waters will leap in with both feet. Some begin with modest reflection on evidence they already have at hand (that stack of student exams), or with participation in conversations about teaching. In time, those activities may lead to more full-fledged enactments of the process described in this chapter. Though CASTL has used the language of "the project" to describe the work done by scholars of teaching and learning, it is perhaps better described as a set of habits and commitments that come into play in different combinations and levels of ambition throughout a faculty member's career.

This description, we are well aware, stretches the envelope of the scholarship of teaching and learning. And some readers will certainly object, concerned that such a broad view puts the status and dignity of the work at risk, reinforcing concerns about whether the work is "too soft" to be seen as real research, or, for that matter, to guide improvement efforts reliably.

We understand these concerns. The place of this kind of scholarship in the reward system may well depend—especially in more research-oriented settings—on hewing to a narrower definition that closely parallels the features of traditional scholarship and leads to traditional forms of publication. Yet all serious scholarly enterprises have and *need* this range to be successful. That is, intellectual and professional habits, on the one hand, and more formal features of traditional scholarship and publication, on the other, necessarily underwrite and reinforce each other; an intellectual field or pursuit cannot flourish without both (or without the full range of engagement between these extremes).[11] Moreover, if the scholarship of teaching and learning is to be something more than a special area in the research of a few faculty, if it is to influence and improve the work in large numbers of classrooms, it needs, as we say in Chapter One, a big tent where there is space for small-scale efforts aimed mostly at local improvement as well as more ambitious, sustained work of larger scale. The key, in fact, is not the scale and scope but the care and thoughtfulness of the work, its capacity to change thought and practice, its generativity, even, perhaps, its power to surprise and delight. These are not, it should be said, soft standards but rigorous demands appropriate to the purposes and character of the work.

The Promise of the Teaching Commons

As we end this chapter, it is useful perhaps to reiterate that the scholarship of teaching and learning is not new. There have been groups of faculty who have made systematic work on pedagogy a central aspect of their careers for decades, and those who have come more recently to the work owe these earlier pioneers a debt of gratitude. What is *new* is the realization that scholars from across the full range of disciplines and professional fields can productively engage with pedagogical questions. Whereas educational research has traditionally been the province of faculty in schools or departments of education, or education specialists in some disciplines, the scholarship of teaching and learning invites involvement by faculty across the full spectrum of research specialties and fields.

This invitation is not without its challenges. Faculty in most disciplines have no formal training in the kind of work we are talking about. Indeed, they often have no training in teaching itself. For the scholarship of teaching and learning to deliver on its promises, campuses (and graduate schools) will need to become places that can nurture and support this work through appropriate programs, structures, and rewards. Scholarly and professional societies will need to develop top-notch journals, conferences, special events, and standards to advance it. As we will report in later chapters, there is still much to be done to meet these needs, but significant progress has been made.

In our view, some of the most important progress comes in the form of visions and images of what the future might look like if the scholarship of teaching and learning delivers fully on its promises. In an essay on teaching and scholarship in her field, sociologist Carla Howery ends with what she calls her "I have a dream speech." Imagine, she invites her readers, that discussants at professional meetings would routinely ask presenters: "What are the implications of this material for undergraduate education and how would you teach it?" Imagine "inspiring metrics for teaching excellence at *each* faculty rank," and that "national associations would be called on to recommend peer reviewers of teaching products" (Howery, 2002, pp. 155–156). Similarly, Stanford English professor Andrea Lunsford, writing to colleagues in a national initiative on the doctorate, imagines a world in which "graduate students are colleagues rather than acolytes, our partners in exploring major issues, in constructing new knowledge, and in sharing the wealth of our experiences, our learning, and our teaching." In such an atmosphere, she says, "a focus on pedagogy would be right and necessary," and graduate programs would develop "ongoing teaching/pedagogy circles that would include faculty, staff, and graduate students, again working collaboratively" (Lunsford, 2006).

Lunsford does not use the language of the scholarship of teaching and learning, but her vision captures, in miniature, the promise of a teaching commons to which such work can contribute and from which it can benefit. It is not, of course, a physical place but rather an intellectual space, characterized by what Corynne McSherry calls an "ethic of sharing" (2001, p. 17), where ideas, practices, products, and (to use the language now popular in educational technology circles) learning and teaching objects can be made available, known, and built on. In an important essay on course portfolios, Dan Bernstein muses about the difference such a space would make:

> To me the most important benefit of creating a community [around teaching and learning] is that we no longer lose a great deal of intellectual work that is regularly being done. Talented people find ingenious solutions to problems in learning every academic term, and traditionally most of that work is lost. When people know that there is a community of people who will look at their work, especially the cumulative intellectual work of several offerings of a course, they will

> be willing to take the modest extra steps of recording and reflecting on what they are already accomplishing as teachers. As a result there will be a large community of teachers whose decisions about how to teach will be informed by the collective effectiveness of the work. [Bernstein, 2001, pp. 228–229]

This powerful vision captures the possibilities of the scholarship of teaching and learning as it has evolved over recent years. The teaching commons that is now being built by growing numbers of faculty engaged in such work makes real breakthroughs in teaching and learning more likely than ever before. In such a space, conversation about teaching and learning—informed by evidence and grounded in practice—can become the norm rather than the exception. Disciplines can engage in active trading of ideas about pedagogy. Ways of sharing and citing one another's work will emerge and become commonplace. And faculty will stand on the shoulders of others who have gone before.

NOTES

1. This epigraph is from "The Scholarship of Teaching and Learning," by Eileen Bender and Donald Gray (1999). Bender and Gray's piece introduces a collection of essays about scholars of teaching and learning at Indiana University. Indiana embraced the scholarship of teaching and learning early on, and has developed an extensive campus program that won the nationally competitive Hesburgh Award for faculty development in 2003.
2. Action research takes place in many sites, in each of which it has different roots and meanings. In K–12 settings, where it is variously known as *classroom action research, teacher research,* or *practitioner research,* it generally "involves the use of qualitative, interpretive modes of inquiry and data collection by teachers [often with help from academics] with a view to teachers' making judgments about how to improve their own practices" (Kemmis and McTaggart, 2000, p. 569). For a review of its recent past and future prospects in schools, professional development programs, and teacher education, see Cochran-Smith and Lytle, 1999. Often seen as a way to engage classroom teachers with academic discourse on teaching and learning, action research has generated much discussion about relationships between educators in the schools and in colleges and universities, and the different kinds of knowledge they generate, value, and use (see, for example, Coulter, 1999; Anderson and Herr, 1999; Ellis, 1997). The scholarship of teaching and learning in higher education may bear a family resemblance to action research, but its emphasis on faculty

using their own disciplines and research styles to pursue classroom inquiry is different, as are its tensions and problems.

3. Numerous definitions have been floated out onto higher education's waters. Carnegie's own publications on the topic have, in fact, told an evolving story, moving from the very broad definition in the 1990 report *Scholarship Reconsidered* (see Chapter One of this volume), to more pointed ones in later statements. For instance, in a 1999 *Change* magazine article, Hutchings and Shulman propose distinctions among teaching well, scholarly teaching, and the scholarship of teaching and learning. Although these distinctions have been found useful by many, and we have built on them, we believe there is an argument to be made for a more inclusive view.
4. The image of standing on the shoulders of giants is usually traced to Newton, but its longer history is delightfully documented in Robert Merton's *On the Shoulders of Giants* (1993). For an additional spin on the idea, take a look at *The Rule of Four,* a novel whose main characters are writing senior theses at Princeton University. One of those characters, Paul, tells his roommate about the assistance he received from friends and mentors in solving the puzzle to a Renaissance text he has been writing about: "Only a man who sees giants," he says, "can ever stand upon their shoulders" (Caldwell and Thomason, 2004, p. 276). The point is nicely relevant to the themes of this volume as well, where knowing there are others "out there" doing significant intellectual work on teaching and learning is a prerequisite to serious engagement with the teaching commons.
5. Concerns about students as human subjects have been on the rise for several years now—part of a more general trend toward increased vigilance by institutional review boards (IRBs). An informal survey of CASTL Scholars in 2001 showed that on a majority of campuses it was "a given" that scholarship of teaching and learning projects should go through the IRB. For faculty from fields that do not usually encounter issues related to the protection of human subjects, this has meant an additional hurdle and learning curve, but the process can also be helpful in raising awareness about the role of students in the scholarship of teaching and learning. As documented in a 2002 Carnegie Foundation publication, *Ethics of Inquiry,* many faculty are involving their students as active participants and collaborators in the scholarship of teaching and learning. For further discussion, including case studies and commentary, see that publication (Hutchings, 2002).
6. For instance, Jacobs has been looking at the role of community-based (or service) learning in the chemistry curriculum. He has also worked with a colleague to develop "TextRev," an initiative examining how students use

and value textbook resources. For more information, visit http://www.textrev.com.

7. For a "taxonomy of questions" in the scholarship of teaching and learning, see the introduction to *Opening Lines: Approaches to the Scholarship of Teaching and Learning* (Hutchings, 2000).

8. Stephen Ehrmann, director of a national project on technology and teaching, proposes that what is needed for the scholarship of teaching and learning is an embrace of "useful uncertainty" (Ehrmann, 2002). The point aligns nicely with Randy Bass's discussion of teaching "problems" as an entrée to such work.

9. It is worth quoting the fuller passage by Schön, which goes as follows: "There is a high, hard ground overlooking a swamp. On the high ground, manageable problems lend themselves to solution through the use of research-based theory and technique. In the swampy lowlands, problems are messy and confusing and incapable of technical solution. The irony of this situation is that the problems of the high ground tend to be relatively unimportant to individuals or to the society at large, however great their technical interest may be, while in the swamp lie the problems of greater human concern" (1995, p. 28).

10. See the H-Teach Web site at http://www.h-net.org/~teach/. These strategies are described in Hutchings's 1996 volume from the American Association for Higher Education, *Making Teaching Community Property.*

11. We are indebted to Randy Bass for this point about the symbiosis between different levels of engagement in all kinds of intellectual and scholarly work.

3

MAPPING THE COMMONS

One of the central ways we make sense of experience is by making differences. The world presents itself without inherent order, and our impulse is to place things in piles, count them, and name them. In the act of creation, day is divided from night. Aristotle classifies just about everything. Shakespeare gives us the seven ages of man, Dante maps the circles of hell, Burton anatomizes melancholy. In ways that Kant never intended by the phrase, we are driven by a "categorical imperative," the irresistible impulse to place things in categories.[1]

CONTRIBUTIONS TO THE COMMONS by scholars of teaching and learning pose exciting possibilities for exchange. As the commons takes shape, faculty exploring new approaches in the classroom can increasingly find like-minded colleagues and useful resources to support their efforts. Scholars of teaching and learning whose projects and investigations produce results that others might find useful are further motivated by the likelihood that their work will find an audience, be enriched by colleagues' comments and critique, and contribute to a larger community of thought and practice. What such a commons makes possible for teaching and learning is, we believe, deeply intriguing, hope giving, and worthy of investment of faculty time and institutional resources. But it is not simple.

The work of teaching occurs in an almost infinite set of contexts—contexts defined by discipline, student demographics, institutional type, pedagogical approach, and curricular goals, to name just a few of the elements whose permutations distinguish one classroom from another. Scholars of teaching and learning deliberately keep their focus close to the classroom, seeking to preserve the particulars of practice. One does not, after all, teach students in general or content in general, but, say, calculus to students who will go on to teach mathematics to our nation's children, or the structure of the cell to students who will take only one biology course. As Kenneth Eble observes in his 1988 classic study, *The Craft of Teaching,* "It is attention to particulars that brings any craft or art to a high degree of development" (p. 6). As the examples we provide in this chapter show, the scholarship of teaching and learning's special role is to concentrate attention on pedagogical particulars and allow others to learn from them.

This attention to context gives the scholarship of teaching and learning much of its richness, and distinguishes it from most (though not all) general or basic research on learning and teaching. As more of this work enters the commons, however, its focus on particular classrooms is beginning to pose a significant conceptual challenge. If the commons is to be something other than a wilderness of unrelated projects and efforts, the work within it must yield to Shulman's version of the categorical imperative. An important task, then, is to identify categories around which the work converges, which can in turn provide maps for traversing and using the commons.

As the scholarship of teaching and learning grows both in the United States and abroad, this mapping task has been much on our minds. In our work with the Carnegie Academy for the Scholarship of Teaching and Learning, for example, we have watched CASTL Scholars from over twenty different fields and all types of institutions frame questions about learning in their particular contexts and explore those questions in myriad ways. Getting to know these people and projects, one by one, has been a great pleasure and privilege. At the same time, we have seen our role as cartographers, regularly stepping back from our engagement with the CASTL participants' particular projects in an effort to discern larger contours of the terrain, looking for themes and questions around which their efforts and those of many others seem to converge.

Examples of the Work

We have already introduced the scholarship of teaching and learning through an example drawn from the work of Dennis Jacobs at Notre Dame. In this chapter, we present five additional examples of the scholarship of teaching and learning from others in the CASTL program. We use them, in part, to highlight that aspect of this pedagogical work that is new: "regular" faculty framing and systematically investigating questions about teaching and learning in their own classrooms. More specifically, we feature these five because their efforts too have sparked the interest of many people we have shared them with, and because, all together, they provide a window into the varied themes and methods that characterize the scholarship of teaching and learning, and thus an opportunity to map out important features of the commons as it evolves.

We look first at the five new examples, then return at the end of the chapter to the mapping task. Along the way we hope these examples will put more meat on the bones of the concept of the scholarship of teaching and learning presented in the previous chapter. We hope, too, that they will begin to answer the question we are often asked: What are the results of all this work? What can others learn from it? In Chapter One, we noted that Dennis Jacobs's project produced evidence on the effectiveness of a new way of teaching chemistry to at-risk students. The examples presented here have contributed to (among other things) a taxonomy of mathematical knowledge for pedagogical purposes, a typology of the ways students use history in political action projects, a theory of intellectual community in seminar courses, strategies to help students deal with difficulty in literary texts, and ways of engaging science-averse students with the concept of the cell in a biology course. These results are improving learning in the classrooms in which they were generated. Some have already made a difference in other classrooms as well.

Example 1: Learning to Think Like a Mathematician

Though they have become a kind of whipping boy for many of the ills facing higher education today, the disciplines are powerful tools for understanding the world. They are where most faculty "live," their primary intellectual home, and the source of some of their most deeply felt hopes for student learning. Not surprisingly, then, the disciplines (and interdisciplines) are also the source of many of the questions explored by scholars of teaching and learning. How do students come to understand key concepts in the field? How do they employ those concepts to make sense of new information and ideas? How do students learn to think like, say, a historian or a physicist? Consider, as a case of the scholarship of teaching and learning focused on disciplinary understanding, the work of Curtis Bennett, a mathematician who has taught at Bowling Green University in Ohio, Michigan State University, and Loyola Marymount University in Los Angeles.[2]

Bennett is a theoretical mathematician, but many of his students are preparing for something very practical: to teach secondary school. He is particularly concerned that these students grasp not only the mechanics and procedures of the discipline but its underlying principles, and what Joseph Schwab called the *syntax* of the field (1964). In particular, he wants students to understand—and therefore be able to teach *their* future students—"what makes a good mathematical question." He wants them to appreciate "the beauty and elegance of a good mathematical proof." As he describes in a course portfolio documenting his efforts to meet these goals in a senior capstone course, "Even though the students in the course were above average, few of them understood what mathematics was. . . . A result of this was that the students treated work in the course as a set of hoops they needed to jump through" (2002, p. 2). Math problems, these future teachers believed, were puzzles that could be solved in five minutes or not at all.

With this challenge in view, Bennett redesigned the course around semester-long, open-ended mathematical research projects intended to challenge students' assumptions about what it means to do math. In groups of two or three, he explains, "Students answered complicated mathematical questions that forced them to confront issues their coursework never led them to before. For example, they needed to create definitions, to refine mathematical problems, and to become owners and creators of mathematics" (2002, p. 2). To track the impact of this new approach, Bennett administered surveys of student attitudes toward mathematics before and after taking the class, kept a journal, copied and analyzed all graded homework assignments and exams, taped and analyzed office-hour conversations with student project groups, and conducted interviews with individual students after final grades were turned in. His scholarship of teaching and learning thus entailed a careful, multidimensional examination of the impact of a new approach on the learning of students.

What did Bennett discover? What insights does his work contribute to the teaching of mathematics? For starters (again, as documented in his course portfolio), he found that the new approach led students to "a more mathematical view" of the work of the field, and, in particular, of what makes a good mathematical problem. But equally important, Bennett asserts, is the way the work brought to light important *next* questions about student learning, especially because "mathematicians judge the value of a question by what it leads to" (Curtis Bennett, interview with the authors, October 22, 2004).

Building on what he learned about students' mathematical understandings, Bennett has moved to a next stage in his investigation, looking at a larger body of evidence with new questions in view, and, importantly, working with a departmental colleague at Loyola Marymount, Jackie Dewar (Bennett and Dewar, 2004b). Together, the two are studying how students grow in their view of mathematical reasoning and argumentation as they move from a freshman workshop course into more advanced work in the major—focusing especially on "what moves students from a reliance on examples to an understanding of and desire for proof" (Bennett and Dewar, 2004a, p. 1). This second project has taken the mathematicians beyond their own setting and discipline into the wider world of educational research. Building on work in cognitive psychology, they have adapted the think-aloud research tool to develop a "proof-aloud protocol" for probing students' thinking, in which they ask students to investigate a number theory statement, say how confident they are about their conclusions and what would make them more confident, write a proof for their conclusions, and discuss what mathematics learning they drew on for these tasks.

As Bennett and Dewar grappled with characterizing students' development in mathematical understanding, they also turned to the literature on assessment. "We needed a more nuanced way to describe the progression of our students' understanding," Dewar explains (Jackie Dewar, interview with the authors, October 22, 2004). In the end, they adapted a framework for assessing student learning by Stanford University professor of education Richard Shavelson (see Shavelson and Huang, 2003),[3] overlaid it with a model of student progression from novice toward expert (Alexander, 2003), and reframed the whole to meet their own purposes and needs. (See Exhibit 3.1.)

The result is a *mathematical knowledge expertise grid* that they and other mathematicians can use for targeting instruction and that gives language for describing critical aspects of student learning in mathematics (Bennett and Dewar, 2004a). It is also, not incidentally, a nice example of how efforts from different communities inside the bigger tent of the scholarship of teaching and learning can converge to create something new.

Example 2: From Historical Understanding to Political Action

We have been struck by how many faculty come to the scholarship of teaching and learning as a way of raising questions about the fundamental purposes of higher education: the "access to what?" issue. Beyond disciplinary understandings—the sort of learning Bennett and Dewar are most focused on—they want to know whether and how students apply academic content and skills to contexts that require judgment, action, and commitment. In particular, they have questions about students' moral and ethical development, values related to social justice, and preparation for participation in a democratic society. This set of goals, although often

Exhibit 3.1. Bennett and Dewar Taxonomy of Mathematical Knowledge Expertise

Affective	Acclimation	Competence	Proficiency
Interest	Students are motivated to learn by external (often grade-oriented) reasons that lack any direct link to the field of study in general. Students have greater interest in concrete problems and special cases than abstract or general results.	Students are motivated by both internal (that is, they are intrigued by the problem) and external reasons. Students still prefer concrete concepts to abstractions, even if the abstraction is more useful.	Students have both internal and external motivation. Internal motivation comes from an interest in the problems from the field, not just applications. Students appreciate both concrete and abstract results.
Confidence	Students are unlikely to spend more than five minutes on a problem if they cannot solve it. Students don't try a new approach if first approach fails. When given a derivation or proof, they want minor steps explained. They rarely complete problems requiring a combination of steps.	Students spend more time on problems. They often spend more than five minutes on a problem before quitting and seeking external help. They may consider a second approach. They are more comfortable accepting proofs with some steps "left to the reader" if they have some experience with the missing details. They can start multistep problems but may have trouble completing them.	Students will spend a great deal of time on a problem and try more than one approach before going to text or instructor. Students will disbelieve answers in the back of the book if the answer disagrees with something they feel they have done correctly. Students are accustomed to filling in the details of a proof. They can solve multistep problems.
Cognitive	**Acclimation**	**Competence**	**Proficiency**
Factual	Students start to become aware of basic facts about the topic.	Students have working knowledge of the facts of the topic, but may struggle to access the knowledge.	Students have quick access to and broad knowledge about the topic.
Procedural	Students start to become aware of basic procedures. They begin to mimic procedures from the text.	Students have working knowledge of the main procedures. They can access them without referencing the text, but may make errors or have difficulty with more complex procedures.	Students can use procedures without reference to external sources or difficulty. Students are able to fill in missing steps in procedures.

Schematic	Students begin to combine facts and procedures into packets. They use surface level features to form schema.	Students have working packets of knowledge that tie together ideas with common theme, method, and/or proof.	Students have put knowledge together in packets that correspond to common theme, method, or proof, together with an understanding of the method.
Strategic	Students use surface level features of problems to choose between schema, or they apply the most recent method.	Students choose schema to apply based on just a few heuristic strategies. Students are slow to abandon a nonproductive approach.	Students choose schema to apply based on many different heuristic strategies. Students self-monitor and abandon a nonproductive approach for an alternate.
Epistemic	Students begin to understand what constitutes evidence in the field. They begin to recognize that a valid proof cannot have a counterexample. They are likely to believe based on five examples; however, they may be skeptical.	Students are more strongly aware that a valid proof cannot have counterexamples. They use examples to decide on the truth of a statement but require a proof for certainty.	Students recognize that proofs don't have counterexamples, are distrustful of five examples, see that general proofs apply to special cases, and are more likely to use "hedging" words to describe statements they suspect to be true but have not yet verified.
Social	Students will struggle to write a proof and include more algebra or computations than words. Only partial sentences will be written, even if they say full sentences. Variables will seldom be defined, and proofs lack logical connectors.	Students are likely to use an informal shorthand that can be read like sentences for writing a proof. They may employ connectors, but writing lacks clarity often due to reliance on pronouns or inappropriate use or lack of mathematical terminology.	Students write proofs using complete sentences that are clear and concise. They employ correct terminology and are careful to define variables.

more a matter of hope than of explicitly pursued outcomes for student learning, is a focus of important work on a growing number of campuses (Colby, Ehrlich, Beaumont, and Stephens, 2003). A concern with social responsibility and civic engagement is also a centerpiece in our next example of the scholarship of teaching and learning by two faculty members from the California State University-Monterey Bay, Gerald Shenk and David Takacs.

At CSUMB, cultivating social responsibility and the skills needed for community building is part of the campus vision and a goal for all students' learning (California State University-Monterey Bay, 1994). Fully committed to this goal, and recognizing the challenge it represents, Shenk, a historian, and Takacs, whose field is environmental humanities, set out to learn more about how their course, the Social and Environmental History of California, moves students toward meaningful engagement with community issues.

Central to the aims of the course is a culminating assignment called the Historically Informed Political Project (HIPP). As the syllabus makes clear (and learning this is one of the important goals of the course), *political* is meant as a broad category: "Any activity is political if it affects how people in a society govern themselves." Thus, students are told, the HIPP must reflect "your own personal values and assumptions about the world you live in," and incorporate "historical research that helps you understand the background of your project"; it also requires at least ten hours of community experience related to the project (Shenk and Takacs, 2000, p. 1). To meet these requirements, three students worked together to campaign for a local initiative to create an urban growth boundary, controlling suburban sprawl around the small town of Marina, California. Another student attempted to bring together various interested parties to address the problem of silting in the Salinas River (Shenk, 2001b).

The HIPP is a daunting assignment for students, and the instructors' questions about it are similarly ambitious: "Do students show a more sophisticated understanding of politics as a result of doing the work for our course? Do they have a firmer grasp of policy issues? Do they express empowerment about making a difference in their communities? Do they show a commitment to continue their work? Do they develop a sophisticated understanding of the connection between values and politics?" (Takacs, 2002, p. 27). Because the course fulfills a California State University system requirement related to California history (and because, after all, it *is* a history course), Takacs and Shenk also want to know what students learn about history.

At the end of the semester, when they collected the HIPP reports and sat down to read them, it was this last question that caught the attention of the two. "I'm a historian," Shenk says, "and my first response was that we didn't do a good job of teaching history." They saw the scholarship of teaching and learning as an invitation, then, to look more closely at students' work, to ascertain whether and why this might be so (Shenk, 2001a). Further, this more careful examination entailed an important shift, which "changed everything" (Shenk, 2001a): rather than focusing on what students did *not* do, Shenk and Takacs decided to look at what their students *did* do—at how, exactly, they *used* history in their political projects. This would help the instructors design strategies to assist students to become more sophisticated in their grasp of the historical underpinnings of contemporary community issues.

Takacs and Shenk began by reading through all the HIPP reports again. What they found was that some students identified historical themes that helped define their projects. Some analyzed historical documents or artifacts that bore on the project. Working inductively from what students had done, they eventually developed a list of ten ways of using history—a taxonomy (as they call it) that then served as a tool for more carefully identifying and analyzing the elements of students' learning as they moved from historical understanding to political action. (See Exhibit 3.2.)

The most important result of the project is arguably the taxonomy itself, because it is something other faculty can build on and use in their own scholarship of teaching and learning. In addition, the project led to new insights about how students connect their own values with historical understanding. For starters, Takacs explains, they found that when students connect their personal lives in a deep way to the larger historical and political themes of their projects, the quality of the work improves. "When they get to design projects around an issue that they care about, they are much more likely to be invested in the scholarly work that helps situate that project. It's not just an arid term paper: it's something they come to want to understand" (David Takacs, e-mails to the authors, October 5 and November 2, 2004). The two scholars have also begun to identify aspects of personal and cognitive development that affect this kind of engagement, finding that older students, with more life experience, are more likely to connect the personal and the academic in meaningful ways. Assisting younger students in such work may require more explicit scaffolding and "guiderails," as Takacs calls them.

Takacs and Shenk have shared findings from the project with colleagues at CSUMB as part of a scholarship of teaching and learning collaborative, and also with fellow historians through *Perspectives,* a publication of the American Historical Association (Shenk and Takacs, 2002). Further, they

Exhibit 3.2. Takacs and Shenk Taxonomy of Students' Uses of Historical Research to Inform Political Projects

1. They identify historical themes that help them situate their political action.
2. They deconstruct systems of power so that they can understand the institutions they are trying to change or conserve.
3. They analyze historical evidence, documents, or artifacts whose meanings help them understand the meaning of the current-day political work they are doing.
4. They situate themselves as actors in history, explicitly examining their actions as part of a historical stream.
5. They see themselves as products of history, explicitly situating themselves as resulting in some way from a stream of historical events, persons, or institutions.
6. They situate their political work as part of a chronology of events.
7. They situate their political work as part of a chain of events, in which they are the next link in the chain.
8. They use historical events to make analogies with their current-day issues of concern.
9. They use history to derive parables about their current-day issues of concern.
10. They use their own personal history to help understand their own political actions.

have used what they learned to catalyze a next stage of teaching and inquiry and to connect with faculty at other colleges and universities who, as part of another Carnegie project, are also making systematic efforts to strengthen students' political understanding and engagement.

Example 3: Intellectual Community in an Interdisciplinary Seminar

One of the pedagogical approaches most closely identified with liberal education is the seminar. Virtually all campuses offer seminars, and for many faculty the image of a small group of students around a table grappling with seminal texts and ideas captures something quintessential about the educational experience (Gale, 2004). But such settings make high demands on learners, and on teachers, too; the seminar is unlikely to deliver on its promises unless a special kind of intellectual community is developed. How does that happen? What does it look like? These are among the questions that propelled psychologist Jose Feito, a faculty member at Saint Mary's College of California, into the scholarship of teaching and learning.

At Saint Mary's all students take a four-semester "Great Books" sequence of seminars, loosely modeled on the program at St. John's College.[4] Having himself had an intensive seminar experience as an undergraduate at the University of Chicago, Feito was delighted to have found a position on a campus that embraced the method and used it extensively. And he was pleased to find among his Saint Mary's colleagues considerable thoughtfulness about "best practices" in seminar classes, especially around the development of rhetorical and critical thinking skills (2002, p. 1). At the same time, he found his own interests moving in a slightly different direction. "As a social psychologist," he writes, "I am curious about how students learn in cooperative and communal classroom environments" and how the pedagogy of the seminar "can strengthen values of interdependence and mutual respect among students commonly conditioned to self-serving, individualist perspectives on education" (2001b, p. 1). Using as a lab his Greek Thought and Literature seminar, the first of the four courses in Saint Mary's required sequence, Feito set out to explore these questions.

Like many scholars of teaching and learning—indeed, like scholars in any arena—Feito found that his questions shifted as he moved into the work of exploration. At first, he says, "I had hoped that my Carnegie project could help me to lead a 'better seminar'; one that could meet these lofty objectives [of building intellectual community] more consistently and efficiently." But soon enough he realized that he "did not have a sufficiently articulated theory of what intellectual community in fact *was*" (Feito, 2002, p. 1). Before he could hope to look at practical questions about the best ways to organize and teach a seminar, he needed a conceptual framework for looking at the dynamics of such courses. As luck would have it, during the semester he began his project he had a particularly engaged and thoughtful group of students, who developed precisely the kinds of interdependence and community he was hoping to explore.

Feito's approach took several directions. First, because he was especially interested in how students themselves experience the seminar, he developed a simple survey, which he administered several times during the semester, asking students to respond to a set of statements about the previous seminar session: "We had a valuable and productive discussion." "I learned from my classmates during the discussion." "Our discussion increased my understanding of the text" (Feito, 2001a). Responses to statements like these gave Feito access to students' perceptions of seminar dynamics.

He was interested not only in students' perceptions but in what actually *happened* during the seminar: who talked to whom, how often, what rhetorical "moves" occurred when discussion was especially lively or productive, how patterns of interaction changed over time. Armed with a small digital tape recorder and permission from students, he recorded thirteen ninety-minute class sessions, created MS Word files from the digital recordings, and then used qualitative research software to code the transcripts based on interpretive categories derived from his students' own words. Though he had not done this kind of discourse analysis before, the process of creating a code to analyze behavior was familiar to Feito as a social psychologist. Like many scholars of teaching and learning, he was bringing the scholarly tools of his discipline to questions raised by his teaching.

What did he learn? In keeping with his interest in developing "a theory of what intellectual community actually *was*," Feito's findings come primarily in the form of themes or features that constitute the experience of intellectual community in a seminar. One such theme—one that particularly captured the imagination of Feito's fellow CASTL Scholars—is what he calls "intellectual intimacy," a dynamic in which students come to know one another's thoughts and ideas in ways they may not in their "day-to-day friendships." The seminar, in Feito's view, becomes a special space where a different, and in some ways deeper, intellectual form of intimacy develops (Feito, 2002, p. 5).

Another theme that emerged in Feito's work was what he called "not knowing." "In order for shared inquiry to proceed," he observes, "the participants must acknowledge their initial lack of understanding. They must be willing to say 'I don't know'" (Feito 2002, p. 3). This insight provided the foundation for a next chapter in Feito's scholarship of teaching and learning (and a second successful application to CASTL) focused on how seminar participants learn to allow this kind of not knowing, and what forms it takes. It was also grist for the establishment of a working group on seminar pedagogy—a cluster of projects by scholars from different settings and disciplines who share Feito's interest. One of them is looking at how students learn to ask questions (Greene, 2004); another at how students develop a sense of responsibility for others' learning as well as their own (Ostroff, 2004). Cosponsored by the Carnegie Foundation and the Center of Inquiry in the Liberal Arts at Wabash College, this working group is mapping out the terrain of the seminar in ways that promise to enrich practice in many settings.[5]

Exhibit 3.3. Jose Feito's Facets of Intellectual Community

1. Student ownership
   Students recognize their ownership of the learning process.
   Students are dissatisfied with overly directive instructors.
2. Shared inquiry
   There is an appreciation for the generative potential of multiple perspectives.
   Students are surprised at the insights of "quiet people."
   Students are dissatisfied when other students do not engage.
3. Allowing "not knowing"
   Students have the ability to acknowledge their initial lack of understanding.
   Students have a willingness to be wrong and let their opinions evolve.
   Students ask genuine questions.
   There is space for students to struggle with a difficult text.
4. Socio-emotional climate
   The atmosphere is emotionally safe—students know they will not be attacked.
   There is an expectation of help from fellow students.
   There is mutual encouragement and support.
   There is a perception of shared fate and commonality—"We're all in the same boat."
   Tension is relieved through humor.
5. Intellectual intimacy
   Students have deeper access into the inner workings of one another's minds.
   They know classmates on a more profound level than they know their friends.
   There is permeability to the opinions of others.

Example 4: The Role of Difficulty in Learning

Many faculty resonate with what University of Pittsburgh English professor Mariolina Salvatori recalls from her days as a beginning instructor. "I remember," she says, "feeling impatient with students. . . . I knew I chose demanding texts, but even so I found it frustrating when they would declare, 'This text is too difficult for me' or 'It does not make any sense,' pinning, I thought, the responsibility of making things understandable on the text rather than on themselves" (2000, p. 84). It was in this way that Salvatori realized that the role of difficulty in student learning could become a focus for her pedagogical inquiry: "What counts as difficulty, and how do learners experience it? What forms does it take? Is difficulty a constitutive part of learning? Is there a relationship between difficulty and educational approaches? How do teachers teach students to deal with difficulty? These are important questions for me because the premise of my scholarship of teaching and learning is that 'moments of difficulty' often contain the seeds of understanding" (p. 81).

Not incidentally, they are also important questions in Salvatori's discipline: English studies and its neighboring fields have generated a considerable body of theoretical and empirical research on the process of interpretation and meaning making as readers come to different kinds of texts (see, for instance, Iser, 1978; Steiner, 1978; Salvatori, 1988; Purves, 1991). Salvatori has both drawn from this research and contributed to it, and her project as a CASTL Scholar continues this line of work by looking at the uses and impact of what she calls "the difficulty paper"—an assignment she describes to students as follows:

> You can expect to write regularly in this course. *In preparation for class discussions and writing assignments,* you will write short (1/2 to 1 page) "difficulty papers": these are papers in which you identify and begin to hypothesize the reasons for any possible difficulty you might be experiencing as you read a _______ (a poem, play, or essay). Each week, you will write a difficulty paper on one or more of the assigned texts. Each week, I will select one or two of them as unusual or representative examples of the readings you produce. I will photocopy, distribute, and use them to ground our discussions. My goal, in doing so, is to move all of us from judging a difficulty as a reader's inability to understand a text to discerning in that difficulty a reader's incipient awareness of the particular "demands" imposed by the language/structure/style/content of a text. [Salvatori and Donahue, 2004, p. 9]

This is heady stuff. Indeed, Salvatori talks about the ways this understanding of the reading process requires teaching "against the grain." On the one hand, American academic culture "does not take well to the idea of difficulty," she notes; we value being smart. On the other hand, the most sophisticated scholars, the most "consummate and passionate learners" embrace what can only be called "a cult of difficulty," which sometimes becomes, whether by design or otherwise, a way to exclude novice learners (2000, p. 82; see also Graff, 2003). Salvatori's aim is an egalitarian one: to advance a way of thinking about learning that invites students new to the academic enterprise to find their way from difficulties to deep and satisfying forms of understanding.

Much of Salvatori's work as a scholar of teaching and learning is, then, focused on articulating a theory. The project she did as a CASTL Scholar has an empirical dimension—she examined evidence that would show whether the difficulty paper actually improves students' writing and comprehension. She also worked with colleagues in other humanities fields to help them adapt the assignment to their different circumstances and contexts. She has presented her work in many disciplinary and cross-disciplinary pedagogical venues, where the strategies she has developed to help students make the most of difficulty resonate with faculty from the sciences and social sciences as well.

But Salvatori's primary interest, and in our view the most powerful product of her work, lies in articulating a theory of learning through difficulty. Continuing this work, she has been collaborating with a colleague from another campus—Patricia Donahue, a faculty member in English at Lafayette College—to coauthor a book on difficulty aimed at *students* as well as teachers. The point is that what is good for the teacher to understand about the learning process is also good for the learner. As Salvatori and Donahue explain, something difficult is something that is hard to understand, and it can be hard to understand for different reasons: "because it is perplexing, obscure, mysterious, remote, strange, unfamiliar, uncomfortable, disconnected, meaningless, confusing, ridiculous, contradictory, hypocritical, inconsistent" (2004). Identifying what the reasons are, and engaging with rather than backing away from them, the authors suggest to student readers, is an important step in handling difficult texts—and also, we would add, other puzzling phenomena in life as well as in school.

Example 5: Being at Home in the Cell

Our final example is the work of Maura Flannery, a biologist at Saint John's University (New York). One of Flannery's long-standing interests is the aesthetics of biology, and she has written widely about the role of the visual in understanding and representing science—in particular, her passion, the cell. Her Carnegie project, not surprisingly, had its roots in this interest; her intent was to investigate "how students come to understand images of cells and molecules" and how visual images affect their understandings (2000, p. 1). As the project progressed, however, its focus shifted:

> I decided that the central question I wanted to explore in my class was: What does it mean to be at home in the cell? I saw this question as intimately involving the visual. The only way we really know the cell is through visual images, since we can't actually visit a cell. I liked this question because I think it has affective as well as cognitive aspects.

> To be "at home," implies that you feel comfortable, and one of my major aims in teaching non-majors is to get them to feel more comfortable with science, to have a better attitude toward science. Also, to be at home means being someplace you know well, you know your way around it, and you know how it "works" in the sense of where to turn on the heat and how to turn on the faucet in the shower. So being at home in the cell also has a cognitive aspect: knowing the parts of the cell, where they are in relation to each other, and how they work. [2001c, p. 1]

This interest in the cell as home, and home as a place where cognitive and affective understandings come together, is, though quite personal for Flannery, not idiosyncratic. Indeed, "the idea of thinking and feeling as closely linked is receiving more attention," she notes, citing Antonio Damasio's *Descartes' Error* (1994), and the work of Robert and Michele Root-Bernstein (2000), who have written on the importance, especially for scientists, of thinking with emotion. She has, she says, "long been interested in what Gerald Holton (1978) calls the private side of science, the side that deals with how science is really done, the side that includes the passion and intuition of the scientist" (2000, p. 11; see also Flannery, 2001b). This is a side of science Flannery wants to share with her own students—students who are not likely to major in science and who often find it intimidating and strange.

Although, we suspect, many science faculty would agree that this is a noble aim, it is not the principle that drives their classroom teaching, where issues of coverage are likely to dominate and where assessment focuses on facts and knowledge. Flannery admits that her own methods have been shaped by the mainstream disciplinary perspective—for instance, her use of traditional tests and exams. But what she realized as she began her scholarship of teaching and learning project was that she needed windows into her students' learning that could not be provided through traditional assessments and assignments. A central task of her project, then, was to create new ways of uncovering her students' learning. For starters, she designed a simple pretest that asked students at the beginning of the semester about their attitudes toward and knowledge of biology (one of the questions asks, "If you could visit the inside of a cell, what would this experience feel like?") and invited them to draw a cell and a molecule. At the end of the semester, when the task was repeated, she was pleased to see more elaborated images—not only what she calls "the fried egg" image of the cell but more complicated representations that had "sprouted labels" (Flannery, 2001a).

In other attempts to find out more about her students' understanding of biology, Flannery experimented with new writing assignments. Several weeks into the semester, she asked students to write about a place they feel at home. One wrote about being in an electronics store, another about being in her boyfriend's arms. Regardless of the variety of places described, "they used words like peace, quiet, security, and safety," Flannery reports, "words I have used in the past to describe my attraction to 'being' down in the cell." The essays helped Flannery get to know her students at a different level, and also gave her a repertoire of metaphors to "help them see the cell as a place they might like to spend time" (2000, pp. 1–2). At the end of the semester, each student was required to assemble a portfolio including twenty items (newspaper clippings, photographs, images from Web sites, and at least one work of visual art, one piece of music, and one poem) about a sensory experience that could be understood through science. They had to label each item, indicating how it related to the theme, and write a self-reflective essay on what they learned from developing the portfolio.

What did Flannery conclude from her experiments? What lessons or results does she have to report? Modestly, she says, "It's small, a little change. I think my message will be: a little change can mean a lot. This could be an important message for [colleagues, especially] . . . the overworked, the timid, and the aged," she adds, only half-jokingly (2000, p. 3). A scientist, Flannery is careful about the claims she makes, and candidly points out that her classroom experiments did not magically transform the learning of all students. But she has documented important changes involving several of her most cherished goals. "For years," she says, "I've been interested in the relationship of the objective and subjective in science; this semester I've finally managed to help my students make that link." Their portfolios, for instance, show "that students had related biology to things that were important to them, and they had seen that there could be an emotional side to biology" (2001a, p. 6). These do not seem like such small changes to us.

Flannery's experiments with new ways to introduce students to the passionate pursuit of knowledge have captured the attention of her fellow biologists; her CV includes numerous conference sessions and journal articles on the topic. There are like-minded colleagues from disciplines beyond the sciences as well. Sociologist Mona Phillips, for instance, focused her work as a CASTL Scholar on "the *joy* of theorizing"—looking at how she can bring her Spelman College students more fully into the experience of meaning making that is, for her, at the very heart of the discipline (Phillips, 2000).

This interest in the more personal, emotional aspects of teaching and learning has not always found an easy place in scholarly work on pedagogy in higher education. But this stream of work has its own roots and traditions. A growing interest in such matters has made Parker Palmer's work on the "courage to teach" an important influence (1998), and has led some faculty to discover Benjamin Bloom's *other* taxonomy focused on affective development.[6] Eliot Eisner, a longtime scholar and proponent of aesthetic education, puts the imperative behind such work eloquently: "The durable outcomes of schooling are not to be found in short-term, instrumental tasks. If students are not moved by what they study, why would they want to pursue such studies on their own? But one has a hard time keeping them away from things that do provide them with deep satisfactions. Can we aspire for less in education?" (1985, p. 35). Flannery and scholars of teaching and learning who share her passions and interests would clearly answer *no*. Indeed, a new *Journal of Cognitive Affective Learning* has been launched, growing out of a broader community that shares the view that "our intellect rests in the mind and the heart" (Owen-Smith, 2004, p. 11).

Signposts and Markers

As we argue in the previous chapter, one of the problems that propels the scholarship of teaching and learning is that the work of the classroom has tended to be private, or at least local, not readily transferable to other settings. Certainly this challenge is evident in our examples—Dennis Jacobs in Chapter One and the five offered here as well; each is deeply embedded in its particular context. But if teaching and learning are to advance, the commons must be a place where diverse instances and types of work can be connected. Scholars of teaching and learning must be able to find colleagues who share their interests and questions. They must be able to situate their work relative to efforts by others that they can build on and contribute to. But what are the links and common themes that allow these connections? How can the commons be mapped and tapped? What are its signposts and markers?

Disciplinary Questions

One answer evident in all these examples lies in the disciplinary context. Although not all mathematicians teach courses exactly like those that Bennett and Dewar have been studying, they are very likely to share the broad goal of teaching students "to think like a mathematician," and it is easy to see how a group of mathematicians could begin to stake out a territory around this goal, exchanging data, testing each other's conclusions, critiquing one another's work.[7] Similarly, Maura Flannery's work on being at home in the cell is likely to be of special interest to other biologists; Mariolina Salvatori's difficulty paper, though it has been used by faculty in a variety of fields, is likely to find a special reception among colleagues in English who appreciate its theoretical foundations. Lee Shulman has written about "the integrity of the discipline" as an abiding theme in the work of many scholars of teaching and learning. "If one is truly devoted to one's discipline, one is committed to transmitting and developing faithful conceptions and understandings of the discipline in students. Thus the integrity of the discipline leads to a sense of what is best for the students" (2000b, p. 98)—*and,* we would add, to questions that become the basis for the scholarship of teaching and learning. Clearly, one important theme for mapping the teaching commons is the discipline.

Crosscutting Themes

But what is striking, as well, are themes that crosscut and connect diverse disciplines. Jacobs's concern for at-risk students in introductory chemistry is shared by faculty in other sciences who are uneasy about high rates of attrition in their fields (Seymour and Hewitt, 1997). Bennett's interest in thinking like a mathematician and appreciating the beauty of the discipline is echoed in Flannery's commitment to helping her students understand what she calls the private side of science and the aesthetics of biology. Shenk and Takacs, like Flannery, are interested in forms of understanding (in their case, political engagement) that transcend the narrowly cognitive. Salvatori's work on difficulty bears a family resemblance to Feito's work on not knowing. Crosscutting themes like these offer another route into the teaching commons.

Methods and Assignments

Another possibility for mapping the commons lies in the methods that scholars of teaching and learning use to inquire into student learning. Some of these approaches have long pedigrees: the discourse analysis used by Feito, for instance, or the quasi-experimental design that Jacobs was able to use to explore the success of at-risk students in chemistry. In some cases, scholars of teaching and learning have creatively adapted an established method to their own disciplinary and classroom contexts: Bennett and Dewar's "proof-aloud protocol" (from cognitive psychology's "think-alouds") is a case in point. Some of the most interesting methods used by scholars of teaching and learning are carefully designed assignments that can be used for purposes of both instruction *and* inquiry: Takacs and Shenk's Historically Informed Political Project, Salvatori's difficulty paper, and Flannery's pre- and postcourse drawings of the cell come readily to mind. In our experience there is considerable interest in methodological questions, and scholars of teaching and learning seek colleagues in the commons not only based on disciplinary questions and crosscutting themes but also on questions of method.

Evidence

Closely related to methods and assignments is the evidence they produce—evidence that, when made public, is available for others to examine both as a check on the investigator's conclusions and as a source that can be queried with other issues in mind. The achievement and retention data collected by Jacobs are exactly the kind of numerical evidence that many people want to see from the scholarship of teaching and learning—and indeed at Notre Dame these data helped convince faculty in other sciences to give more active, collaborative learning a trial. Other methods, probing more deeply into the processes of student learning, produce different kinds of data—for example, the linguistic and behavioral records generated by Feito for the analysis of student interaction in his seminar, and the transcripts that resulted from Bennett and Dewar's interviews with students. Actual student work on assignments and assessments can be particularly rich grist for discussion among scholars of teaching and learning—and among other students. Recognizing this, Salvatori and Donahue have included (with permission, of course) examples of students' difficulty papers in their book, *The Elements (and Pleasures) of Difficulty* (2004). In the future, the teaching commons may well be a space for collective inquiry using such evidence, where scholars can contribute examples of their own students' work and then treat the larger, shared pool of data as grist for larger lessons and insights (Hatch, Bass, Iiyoshi, and Pointer Mace, 2004).

Analytical Tools

Another signpost that might locate the projects featured in this chapter are the analytical tools these scholars developed for interpreting the evidence they gathered, tools which, though often shaped by the scholar's discipline, offer the promise of portability from field to field. In its early years, CASTL had a song with a refrain that went "make it public, peer-review it, pass it on." What we see from these examples is that the "it" that is passed along in the commons may be results in the sense of evidence and new insights about learning and teaching, but also strategies for interpreting results. Consider, for instance, the taxonomies developed by Takacs and Shenk for how students use history, and by Bennett and Dewar for levels of mathematical understanding. Or one could cite the new conceptual frameworks devised by Feito for examining the seminar and by Salvatori for turning moments of difficulty into opportunities for learning. Tools like these are among the most valuable products of the scholarship of teaching and learning. They focus attention on dimensions of learning that many faculty (and students) had not previously distinguished from one another, help faculty (and students) think more carefully about their goals for a course of study, and serve as catalysts for future work in the teaching commons.

o

When we speak of mapping the commons, we are speaking metaphorically, of course. The signposts and markers we propose here are not particularly fine-grained or discriminating, and certainly we do not mean them to be the final word. Our purpose, rather, is illustrative: to point to a process of mapping that will necessarily evolve over time as more scholars, with more and different interests and lines of work, enter the commons and give it shape. This process is partly an intellectual one, of analyzing and describing the emergent outlines of a field or area of inquiry; it is one in which all fields engage. But the process is also, often, a deeply human one in which individuals who might otherwise be working in isolation find like-minded colleagues, collaborators, coauthors, and working groups that enrich their efforts. As suggested in different ways by each of our examples, the scholarship of teaching and learning leads outward in ways that connect people with new communities and forums for exchange through what Brown and Duguid call "the social life of information" (2000).

Maura Flannery uses the image of home to describe a deep kind of understanding. We would like to borrow and adapt that metaphor as a way of thinking about the shape of the teaching commons. What happens when faculty begin to study their own classrooms might be said to entail a move from home into the larger intellectual agora or marketplace—the commons. Bennett and Dewar move from a focus on their own courses and students to a connection with the work of Richard Shavelson on assessment. Shenk and Takacs go public with their project first in a study group on the scholarship of teaching and learning facilitated by their campus center for teaching, and then beyond campus through their scholarly societies and other larger communities. Mariolina Salvatori's difficulty paper creates lines of exchange with colleagues on her own campus and beyond who borrow it, and whose own work is thus connected to points beyond *their* local setting.

This opening out into a broader intellectual community is, in fact, an important motivation for many scholars of teaching and learning—not just a by-product of the work, but a prime mover. More than half of the participants in Carnegie's program report that their initial involvement in the work was motivated in part by an interest in finding "new colleagues with whom to pursue my interests in teaching and learning." And, happily, almost 75 percent agree or strongly agree that they have indeed found new colleagues (Cox, Huber, and Hutchings, 2004).

What is also interesting is the character of the community that forms around this work. Whether defined by campus context or by discipline, these communities seem to be developing an ethos that sets them apart, for better or worse, from other aspects of academic culture. The difference is illustrated by a story from a microbiologist who has been part of Carnegie's program. She took advantage of her residency at the foundation to get together with San Francisco Bay Area science colleagues she had not seen in some time. In the course of the visit, she described for them what was for her the wonderful process of sharing ideas and shaping one another's projects in the CASTL program. As it turned out, the process of sharing ideas, which she found so engaging, her science colleagues found surprising and risky. Scientists, as she later explained to us, hold their work close in the early stages. Exchange about teaching, in contrast, tends to be open, positive, and supportive.[8] Although these characteristics sometimes make tough criticism hard to get, many faculty find the sense of community around teaching a welcome change from the more competitive ethos of research. As we will see in the next chapter, this sense of community, and the chance to find like-minded colleagues, is an important feature of the pathway that takes faculty into the teaching commons.

NOTES

1. This epigraph comes from Lee S. Shulman's article "Making Differences: A Table of Learning" (2002b, p. 37). "There is no such thing as a 'new' taxonomy," Shulman continues. "All the likely taxonomies have been invented, and in nearly infinite variety. Probably the single most famous list in the world of educational thought is the Taxonomy of Educational Objec-

tives devised by my one-time teacher Benjamin Bloom. I can't begin to talk about a new taxonomy without acknowledging the invaluable contributions of Bloom and his colleagues—as well as other taxonomic pioneers including William Perry, Lawrence Kohlberg, Grant Wiggins, and many others who have attempted to create some system for classifying the kinds of learning we seek for our students" (p. 38). It is interesting to see that scholars of teaching and learning, like those discussed in this chapter, are contributing their own taxonomies to the mix.

2. Bennett applied to the CASTL program in 1998 when he was a faculty member at Bowling Green State University, seeking to explore the impact of innovations he had undertaken on that campus. Then, during the 1999–2000 year, he was a visiting scholar at Michigan State, which thus served as an additional laboratory for his CASTL project. Subsequently, he moved to Loyola Marymount, and, with department colleague Jackie Dewar, applied and was accepted for a second stint as a CASTL Scholar in 2003.
3. This framework appears in "Responding Responsibly to the Frenzy to Assess Learning in Higher Education" (Shavelson and Huang, 2003), though Bennett and Dewar also draw on a version of the framework Shavelson discussed during a visit to their campus. Shavelson and Huang distinguish among several different types of cognitive outcomes, from general ability to domain-specific forms of knowledge. It is the latter that Bennett and Dewar are particularly interested in.
4. St. John's College has two campuses, one in Annapolis, Maryland, another in Santa Fe, New Mexico. As the college Web site says, "There is no other college quite like St. John's" (see http://www.sjca.edu/asp/home.aspx).The undergraduate program is an all-required course of study, taught through seminars on "the great books of the Western Tradition," beginning with the Greeks in freshman year and moving to the twenty-first century in senior year. Students take four years of language, four years of math, three years of laboratory science, and one year of music.
5. CASTL has been partnering with the Center of Inquiry in the Liberal Arts at Wabash College (http://www.liberalarts.wabash.edu/), working toward a better understanding of teaching and learning in liberal education. This collaboration has included a working group focused on the study of the seminar by eight 2003–04 CILA/CASTL Scholars. For information about their work, see http://www.carnegiefoundation.org/KML/KEEP/cases-seminar.htm.
6. Bloom was director of the University of Chicago College Examiner's Office. As a guide for designing assessments, he and his colleagues developed two

taxonomies, one focused on cognitive outcomes (Bloom and Associates, 1956), the other on affective learning (Krathwohl, Bloom, and Masia, 1964). The first has been widely circulated among educators, though much more among K–12 teachers than in higher education, where William Perry's (1970) work is better known. The affective taxonomy is an important complement to the cognitive one. And it is useful to see them together (see Shulman, 2002b, p. 39):

THE COGNITIVE TAXONOMY	THE AFFECTIVE TAXONOMY
Knowledge	Receiving
Comprehension	Responding
Application	Valuing
Analysis	Organizing
Synthesis	Internalizing
Evaluation	

7. Several other CASTL Scholars from math have developed electronic portfolios that explore students' mathematical thinking. See, for instance, http://gallery.carnegiefoundation.org/bcooperstein/, in which Bruce Cooperstein examines work in a course on problem solving that he teaches at the University of California-Santa Cruz. His portfolio was prompted by concerns very like those that shaped Bennett and Dewar's work: "I was moved to initiate this project out of a personal sense that some essential aspects of what it means to 'think mathematically' were missing from my department's overall curriculum. As a consequence, in my view, all too often our students leave the university with the impression that mathematics is a fixed body of knowledge to be memorized rather than a sphere in which they can learn to think for themselves" (Cooperstein, 2000).
8. The "kinder, gentler" culture around teaching and learning may pertain more in the case of cross-disciplinary forums than in conversations about teaching and learning in a single field, where we have seen the more critical culture of disciplinary exchange break through.

4

PATHWAYS INTO THE SCHOLARSHIP OF TEACHING AND LEARNING

About five years ago I became increasingly involved in undergraduate education issues on campus and nationally due to my dismay about the state of biology science education and knowledge at all levels, high school through graduate school. In attempting to understand why the system seems not to work I met wonderful educators from many fields. They helped me change my view of teaching from an activity required as part of my commitment to the university to an area of involvement, creative innovation, and research that is as engaging, challenging, and fun as that of my disciplinary research.[1]

SPENCER BENSON, a biologist at the University of Maryland, introduced himself to his colleagues in the newly selected CASTL class of 2001 with the words we quote in this chapter's epigraph, telling them how he became involved in the scholarship of teaching and learning. His experience had been transformative, but it did not come about through a sudden conversion or flash of insight, and he does not see it as a journey from darkness to light. Instead, like most scholars of teaching and learning, Benson told a story of incremental change. He became more concerned with educational issues, sought to understand the problems better, interacted with people who had similar concerns, increased his involvement in local and national forums and initiatives, and, in the process, rethought his role as a university teacher and his vision of what teaching could mean (see Benson, 2001a, 2001b).

Between the lines of Benson's story is another story of cultural change in his discipline, at his university, and in the wider world of higher education. Whether drawn by concern about education, commitment to students, or curiosity about learning, many faculty are taking a similar journey into the commons, and finding new ways to think about teaching that are more attractive and fruitful than the old. College teaching has often been seen as drawing on gifts or talents quite different from those one cultivates as a professional in one's field (Baker and Zey-Ferrell, 1984; Baker, 1986; Palmer, 1998). But the scholarship of teaching and learning suggests that faculty can enrich and improve their students' learning by also bringing to teaching the habits of intellectual work and inquiry that characterize scholarship in more familiar disciplinary domains.[2] And pioneers like Spencer Benson, who are exploring these possibilities, are finding the change, as he puts it, "engaging, challenging, and fun" (Benson, 2001b).

These new models and scripts for thinking about teaching involve engagement in the professional community of college teachers, and, in fact, many pioneers have become activists for teaching and learning in their own disciplines and on campus. Thanks to their passion and determination, the networks of people aware of such work are becoming larger, denser, and more interconnected, and, as these networks have grown, so too have the structures for professional support. Faculty who start down this road today are increasingly likely to find forums for intellectual exchange about teaching and learning on their campuses and in their disciplines, funding for pedagogical and curricular initiatives, a growing literature about the issues, and opportunities for cross-disciplinary collaboration.

Still, it would be wrong to assume that the current momentum will continue without thoughtful and determined effort. The scholarship of teaching and learning remains a new idea to many faculty members, and in many settings it rubs against the institutional grain, which means that the costs of intensifying attention to teaching and learning can be high. Old certainties about your work as a teacher become problematic,[3] while seriously exploring more promising possibilities means engaging with new literatures, new methods of inquiry, and new colleagues who may know you only through your educational work, not the research on which you have made your reputation. Old colleagues may start questioning your new priorities, and in many settings this means taking risks with the advancement of your career (see Huber, 2002, 2004; Hutchings, 2000). The bottom line is that most faculty are too busy to take up work that is perceived as peripheral to their main responsibilities, gets little recognition, and is not supported or rewarded as a legitimate part of the core.

Given these realities, why *do* college and university faculty become scholars of teaching and learning? What pathways lead people into this work? What communities sustain and support them? The experience of pathfinders as we report it in this chapter suggests that interests in teaching can intensify at any point in an academic career, that the scholarship of teaching and learning is best nurtured through disciplinary ties, and that it is enriched and extended in the "trading zones" that interdisciplinary networks provide. Their experience also affirms the power of joining forces with others in the teaching commons to advocate for change in their various academic communities.

Points of Departure

The first lesson to take from today's scholars of teaching and learning is that most have come to the work through interests in teaching that intensified over time. How those interests developed varies, tracing back to childhood, college, or graduate school for some, but for others not emerging until well into their professional careers. These stories are important, for they suggest the many kinds of programs and opportunities that could help create a world in which scholarly engagement with teaching and learning makes sense.[4]

Although there has been a great deal of excitement in recent years about undergraduate research, there has been less appreciation of the fact that engaging undergraduates in teaching and in educational discussions and debates can be both a formative learning experience for them now and a powerful apprenticeship for a future academic career.[5] For example, Randy Bass of Georgetown University looks back to his college days, when he served three years as student representative on a committee to reform the general education program at his undergraduate institution. Because his college was part of a consortium of colleges concerned with curricular reform, Bass was able to attend national conferences and publish an article in *Liberal Education* on a student's view of the process (1981). During this time, he worked closely with faculty who cared about teaching and learning and watched the reform process go through its entire arc—from a set of exciting ideas to a program only slightly different from what existed before. Characteristically, Bass found this experience eye-opening rather than embittering, and considers it valuable preparation for his subsequent roles as a reformer in the use of new media in humanities education and a national leader in the scholarship of teaching and learning.

Opportunities to develop an interest in teaching and learning multiply during graduate school, because that is where most future faculty actually begin to teach (see Gale and Golde, 2004). Until very recently few graduate programs took this part of professional development seriously, but even without departmental scaffolding, students who are determined or lucky can nourish their pedagogical imagination while working toward a Ph.D. For University of Kansas psychologist Dan Bernstein, who was a graduate student in the late 1960s and early 1970s, the spark came from his dissertation adviser and from a fellow graduate student, whose unconventional views on assessment led to Bernstein's careerlong interest in mastery learning in his own psychology classes.[6] University of Michigan chemist Brian Coppola was funded as a graduate student by research fellowships, but he looked outside his own department for teaching experience. Responding to a call for volunteer tutors, Coppola wound up working with a graduate student in education who introduced him to literature on peer instruction, to methods for classroom observation, and to the benefits of interdisciplinary collaboration in educational research.

Today's graduate students are much more likely to have opportunities built into their graduate training, from formal programs for teaching assistants in their own departments to the national Preparing Future Faculty program, which connects graduate students in doctoral and research universities to departments in nearby undergraduate institutions where they can learn more about the kinds of institutions where most faculty teach. Coppola himself has pioneered a formal program for doctoral students in chemistry at the University of Michigan, where they spend part of their time in their advisers' labs and part on scholarship of teaching and learning projects in the department (Hutchings and Clarke, 2004). When they eventually get faculty positions, they will be able to "hit the ground running," Coppola says (Brian Coppola, interview with the authors, July 15, 2000).

Still, many scholars do not sharpen and intensify their interests in teaching until they have begun their faculty careers—and, for them, campus centers or national initiatives have provided critical opportunities and resources. Roberto Corrada, a law professor at the University of Denver, became engaged in this work when he realized that his labor law students had little in their life experiences or family backgrounds to expose them to labor unions and bargaining. His solution? Seeing a parallel between classroom and workplace, he decided to have his students "unionize" and bargain with him, their professor, on the terms of work—homework, tests, grading policies, and the like. It was only when this process was under way that Corrada joined CASTL's national fellowship program and began reading literature on learning from other fields, exploring the possibilities of technology, evaluating the results, and sharing them more widely with colleagues in his own law school and further afield (Corrada, 2004; see also Corrada, 2001b).

The good news is that this kind of readiness to engage in a more scholarly way with teaching and learning appears to be widespread. Faculty surveys show that most college and university professors care about their students and that they *are* interested in teaching. Indeed, in the Carnegie Foundation's 1997 National Faculty Survey, 71 percent said that undergraduate teaching was very important to them personally. Of course, percentages vary by institutional type, but even at research universities, where most faculty teach graduate students, 54 percent said that undergraduate teaching was very important to them personally; an additional 31 percent said that it was fairly important (Huber, 1998). The challenge, then, is to move faculty to the next steps: to connect questions in their own classrooms to issues of wider concern, engage them with colleagues doing this work, and infuse discussions of teaching and learning with intellectual substance and heft. The key, in other words, is to help faculty see teaching and learning as activities that invite the practices, talents, and passions of scholarship.

Disciplinary Ties

The second lesson to learn from today's scholars of teaching and learning is that the best place to start is where faculty already are, by recognizing their "experience and knowledge of their local context" and "understanding what they are trying to do in their own terms" (Wright, 2003, p. 5).[7] For most faculty, the scholarship of teaching and learning flows from engagement with their own fields. The knowledge practices that faculty are trying to introduce to their students are deeply embedded in their disciplines, and it is often from those disciplines that their best intentions for their students lie. To be sure, as Gerald Graff argues, certain arts of "intellectualizing" crosscut many academic disciplines, such as "the academic faith in the singular virtue of finding problems in subjects . . . the idea that, below their apparent surface, texts harbor deep meanings that cry out for interpretation, analysis, and debate" (2003, p. 46). Yet it is also the case that each field—or family of fields—has its own particular take on such arts as writing, argumentation, problem seeking, and problem solving.

Thus it is that faculty who turn up the heat on teaching and learning are usually drawn by educational agendas that resonate within their own disciplines. Certainly, this is so for the scholars who have populated this chapter so far. For example, Dan Bernstein was intrigued by his dissertation adviser's commitment to "viewing education as a legitimate subject of psychological interest in behavior change. And so, of course, he was interested in the way you teach, and dedicated to the idea that you could do it better, the same way you'd do anything better" (Dan Bernstein, interview with the authors, January 11, 2001). Bernstein's growing interest in mastery learning, then, articulated well with his disciplinary proclivities: his early experimental research on human motivation, his later scholarship of teaching and learning on the construction of exam questions, and his faculty development work on the peer review of teaching have all had a behaviorist's "take" on student learning as a signature theme (Bernstein, 2000; 2001a; see also Huber, 2004).

Randy Bass's fields of literature and American studies did not have as rich a body of pedagogically relevant research as Bernstein's corner of psychology, but Bass found inspiration in neighboring disciplines and their contributions to the growing teaching commons. His dissertation research on documentary narratives of social crisis in nineteenth-century America led him into interdisciplinary efforts to design new media resources that could broaden students' understanding of the period, in particular a multimedia database on Mark Twain and the Mississippi River for middle school students. His later development of new media pedagogies as "engines of inquiry" for undergraduates in the humanities was inspired in part by ideas about writing across the curriculum circulating on the composition side of English (Bass, 1997a, 1997b; see also Huber, 2004).

For scientists, education reform agendas in their own fields come very prominently into play. We have already seen how Spencer Benson's move into the scholarship of teaching and learning began with his growing involvement with issues in biology education. Brian Coppola's first opportunity as a faculty member to focus on issues in chemistry education came through an invitation to help redesign the University of Michigan's undergraduate chemistry curriculum, which subsequently became well-known for its focus on organic rather than physical chemistry, laboratories emphasizing student inquiry, and honors sections with peer instruction (experienced students tutoring novices). Coppola's first forays into the higher realms of the scholarship of teaching and learning came with the need he and his collaborators felt to evaluate the effects these changes were having on their undergraduates and to make their findings available to the larger chemistry community (Ege, Coppola, and Lawton, 1997; Coppola, Ege, and Lawton, 1997; see also Huber, 2004).

Disciplines offer inspiration and direction for the scholarship of teaching and learning, and they also provide the first natural audience for such work, because it is in these communities that one finds colleagues facing the same educational issues. It is chemists, primarily, who are interested in Michigan's focus on organic chemistry as the entrée to the undergraduate chemistry curriculum. Chemists are the first audience for the innovative work done by Coppola and his colleagues on new laboratory experiences for introductory chemistry students. And it is the chemistry community that is most interested in tensions that have formed around the establishment of doctoral programs in chemistry education (see Coppola and Jacobs, 2002). Organizations that fund chemistry research, such as the National Science Foundation, the Research Corporation, and the Camille and Henry Dreyfus Foundation, have supported much of Coppola's educational work. He has presented his views and fought his battles in a wide variety of chemistry forums, including departments of chemistry, the prestigious Gordon Conference on Chemistry Education Research and Practice, sessions organized through the American Chemical Society's Division of Chemical Education, and publications like the *Journal of Chemical Education.*

In fact, education in science, technology, engineering, and mathematics (STEM) has attracted a unique level of national attention and support in the United States because of these disciplines' centrality to defense, health, the environment, and the economy. From 1991 to 2000, for example, the National Research Council's science education committee published reports on undergraduate mathematics (1991), engineering education (1995a), the graduate education and postdoctoral experience of scientists and engineers (1995b, 2000b), the education of mathematics and science teachers (1996b, 1997, 2000a), and undergraduate education in science, technology, engineering, and mathematics (1996a, 1999). In 2004, the National Science Foundation's Division of Undergraduate Education had a budget of $162 million to fund projects on undergraduate education in the STEM fields (R. Haggett, personal communication with the authors, January 3, 2005).

It may not be easy, or even important, to ask how much of this budget went for the scholarship of teaching and learning, as opposed to other contributions to the teaching commons. Still, it is worth noting that a group of leading engineering educators cite the growth of National Science Foundation support for scholarship in engineering education as probably doing "more to raise awareness of the scholarship of teaching and learning in engineering than any other single factor" (Wankat, Felder, Smith, and Oreovicz, 2002, p. 225).[8] Meanwhile, a notable new effort in the sciences is attempting to engage future science faculty in "teaching as research." According to Robert Mathieu, director of the NSF-funded Center for the Integration of Research, Teaching, and Learning, "Our ultimate goal is to develop STEM faculties who themselves continuously inquire into student learning" (n.d., p. 2; see also Center for the Integration of Research, Teaching, and Learning, n.d.).

Although there is less external funding available for teaching and learning initiatives in the social sciences, many of these fields have substantial intellectual capital on which practitioners can draw for understanding the classroom. Psychologists can draw on that field's wealth of theory on learning and cognitive processes (Nummedal, Benson, and Chew, 2002), sociologists can tap into their field's work on race, class, and gender and its understanding of social context (Howery, 2002), management professors can consult the whole subfield of organizational behavior to think about the "classroom as organization" (Bilimoria and Fukami, 2002), and communication scholars can conceptualize "teaching as communication" (Morreale, Applegate, Wulff, and Sprague, 2002). In their scholarly societies, all of these disciplines have active sections focused on education, which organize forums and publish journals in which scholars can present their work.

The humanities, too, provide support for the scholarship of teaching and learning, although in a spottier way. There are fields in which conversations about pedagogy are rich, like composition and humanities-oriented interdisciplinary studies, which came into being in the 1960s and 1970s in response to the challenges of educating a larger and more diverse student population, providing a common experience for entering students, and connecting some of the disconnects between high school and college (Salvatori and Donahue, 2002; Vess and Linkon, 2002). Indeed, it is hardly possible to go to a session at the annual Conference on College Composition and Communication that does not have *something* to do with teaching and learning. Other fields, like English literature and history, have been less open to treating pedagogy as a subject for serious intellectual debate (Salvatori and Donahue, 2002; Calder, Cutler, and Kelly, 2002). As one prominent critic put it, there remains a troubling "refusal of pedagogy" in English literature that blinds many faculty to the intellectual possibilities of the scholarship of teaching and learning, and even to the pedagogical origins of some of its most important methods, like New Criticism's close reading (Guillory, 2002; see also Graff, 1987).[9]

Building disciplinary audiences is a critical challenge for the health and welfare of the scholarship of teaching and learning because the low profile of education in many humanities fields is not unique. Even in the social science and science fields, where discussions of teaching and learning are more robust, the communities of engaged scholars tend to be small and marginalized. Mainstream scholars may look down on those who spend time on educational pursuits of any kind, and scholars of teaching and learning may also find their classroom-based work ignored by colleagues who do larger-scale research on education in their discipline. And it is true that in some disciplinary corners it is a challenge to develop an approach to classroom inquiry that both the scholar in question and his or her colleagues find interesting and sound (see Huber, 2000).

Still, there is energy today around educational issues in many disciplinary communities, which have new or revived outlets that are becoming the context and catalyst for exchange of work on teaching and learning, sites for the development of a common language to talk about pedagogy, and forums for the emergence of shared standards for judging quality (see Table 4.1).

In the world of scholarly societies, these forums include new special interest groups, like the Association for Research in Undergraduate Mathematics Education of the Mathematical Association of America; new journals, like the *Journal of Political Science Education,* recently launched by the American Political Science Association; and new sections of old journals, like "The Scholarship of Teaching and Learning" in *Communication Education,* published by the National Communication Association. Indeed, in some fields, the publication of a pedagogical article in a flagship journal, like David Pace's review essay on history and the scholarship of teaching and learning in *The American Historical Review* (2004), can be seen as a precedent-setting sign of change.[10]

Table 4.1. Changes in Number and Quality of Journals, Articles, and Conference Sessions

	Percent of Respondents			
Changes Seen Over Past Five Years	**No Change**	**Increase in Number**	**Higher Standards**	**Not Sure**
Journals devoted to teaching and learning in my field of study.	45	20	15	7
Articles on the scholarship of teaching and learning in the top journals of my field.	38	29	7	12
Sessions about the scholarship of teaching and learning at the primary annual conference for my field.	19	42	9	13

Source: *Cox, Huber, and Hutchings, CASTL Scholars Survey 2004.*

When talking about developments in the disciplinary neighborhoods of the teaching commons, it is important in these days of the Web to look beyond national borders. In particular, U.S. academics should know about the Subject Network of the Higher Education Teaching Academy, a set of twenty-four subject-specific centers for discipline-based support for learning and teaching in higher education in the United Kingdom. The center for sociology, anthropology, and political science, for example, offers on its Web site news and topics of discussion, resources produced by the center, details of center-sponsored events and workshops, a wealth of subject area materials, including "baseline studies, bibliographies of key texts, Web links, and details of our current projects and activities led by [the center's] academic coordinators," and links to external Web resources (Subject Network for Sociology, Anthropology, and Political Science, n.d.). This is an extraordinary selection of pedagogical information and ideas that can spark the imagination of sociologists, anthropologists, and political scientists anywhere (who have access to the Web).

Developments like these are occurring in many fields now, as faculty gain experience with the scholarship of teaching and learning, both as practitioners in their own right and as knowledgeable audiences for each other's work. The hope, of course, is that discussion will broaden out from forums in which scholars of teaching and learning engage only a few peers, to mainstream journals and conference sessions where a wider range of faculty can learn about the work, engage with more complex and evidence-based treatments of the discipline's educational issues, and join in.

Interdisciplinary Networks

Although disciplinary ties are critical, a third lesson from today's scholars of teaching and learning is the special role of interdisciplinary networks for the collegial care and intellectual feeding of those who engage in this work.[11] Indeed, many who start looking more closely at their own teaching and their students' learning feel as if they are moving *out* of their most familiar scholarly worlds. Their closest colleagues in their disciplinary subspecialties may not be along for the ride, their departmental colleagues may not (yet) be interested. For would-be scholars of teaching and learning, it is often like taking up a new line of work at an oblique angle to what they have done before. This can be exhilarating, not least because it focuses on concerns very close to oneself, but it is often accompanied by anxieties familiar to any scholar venturing into a new intellectual world where conventional disciplinary dispositions do not so clearly pertain.

For parallels, we can look at what happens in other newly developed areas of inquiry before shifts in disciplinary practice are normalized. In anthropology, for example, traditional ethnographic practices have been changing over the past twenty years. Yet, as anthropologist George Marcus notes, it is still the case that exploratory projects into new interdisciplinary areas such as science studies can seem "personal and relatively undisciplined, as not quite anthropology" (1998, p. 242). One can go far with new work, but until its anthropological readership picks up, a "certain accountability" is missing. Without "a sustained discussion among anthropologists . . . the close assessment of arguments and ethnographic claims has been curtailed" (p. 242). In the meantime, however, something is gained because anthropologists engaged in exploratory ethnographic work with new kinds of subjects are finding audiences among colleagues in other disciplines who are viewing that same territory from different points of view.

Interdisciplinary communities are equally important for the scholarship of teaching and learning. For one thing, these communities serve as sanctuaries where people can find friendly critics for their work and with whom they can engage in "corridor talk" about who is doing what, conference opportunities, getting published, finding money, career strategies, and all the other information that is usually passed on informally about the conduct of scholarly work (see Downey, Dumit, and Traweek, 1997). Many of these communities provide opportunities for scholars from across the country to meet face-to-face for several days or more at a time. The prestigious national and regional Lilly conferences bring people together across fields, for example, and the Carnegie Foundation sponsors a series of annual colloquia. Indeed, there are many national—and international—associations and workshops where scholars of teaching and learning can and do meet across disciplines.

Scholars who participate in these events often express relief at being among a group of colleagues with whom they can talk without going back to square one and with whom they can get collectively smarter about pedagogical developments that cross or go beyond subject matter. There is much to be learned about how people in other fields are using new media, for example, or handling the many challenges of designing service-learning experiences that benefit both student learning and the community.[12] And there are also the pleasures of discovering hidden literature: Who in mathematics would know about the journals in, say, chemistry—much less the work of teachers of composition or sociology or theater or law?

Indeed, contemporary scholarship of all kinds is characterized by a growing permeability of disciplinary boundaries, and the scholarship of teaching and learning is no exception. In the commons, people from different disciplines come to find what their own discipline cannot or will not provide (see Huber and Morreale, 2002b). The accounts of scholars of teaching and learning are filled with travelogues of this kind. In redesigning chemistry for at-risk students, Notre Dame chemist Dennis Jacobs borrowed the idea of "concept questions" from Harvard physicist Eric Mazur, learned more about cooperative learning strategies from composition scholar Barbara Walvoord, who was then leading the campus teaching and learning center, and found out about using focus groups for evaluation from other scholars in his CASTL group (Jacobs, 2000).

The concept of academic "trading zones," developed by historian of science Peter Gallison (1997) to explore the sharing of ideas between people from different experimental and theoretical subcultures of high-energy physics, directs attention to interesting features of interdisciplinary exchange in teaching and learning as well. First, it highlights the fact that no single discipline or professional community has a monopoly on the teaching commons. Regardless of their different subjects, methodologies, and histories of attention to teaching and learning, all fields have something to offer and something to gain from trade (see Huber and Morreale, 2002b).

Second, the idea of a trading zone should make us sensitive to the emergence of a common language for trade. Here Gallison's discussion of the pidgins and creoles that develop when people of different cultures come together is especially apropos. Faculty have highly developed vocabularies, or jargons, for discussion of their disciplinary specialties. But when it comes to teaching, few disciplines have made what might best be called their "native pedagogies" fully explicit (see Bourdieu, 1977). Among other things, then, the scholarship of teaching and learning involves an attempt to articulate pedagogical assumptions in order to examine their adequacy and to find ways to scaffold for students the knowledge practices they are expected to master. Talking with faculty from other fields helps scholars find a language that can bring such assumptions and alternatives into the light (see Mills and Huber, 2005).

Third, the trading zone idea highlights the fact that although interdisciplinary trade enriches pedagogical imagination and educational practice, it does *not* mean the loss of disciplinary identities. Yes, those who enter the trading zone may learn a new language that helps them think and speak more clearly about teaching and learning. They may encounter provocative new ideas to bring back to their own classrooms and fields. But this does not mean that the ideas they encounter will travel home unchanged. English professor Mariolina Salvatori's ideas about helping students learn from moments of difficulty have appealed to faculty from the sciences, who themselves have available a suggestive literature on the pedagogical use of student error. But although they may make use of the difficulty paper that Salvatori pioneered for students struggling with poetry, it will look different when it is domesticated into their mathematics or chemistry classrooms. Further, the scientists are not likely to import Salvatori's sources of inspiration, the hermeneutic philosopher Hans-Georg Gadamer (1976), the reader-response theorist Wolfgang Iser (1978), or the many other theoreticians of difficulty in literature on whose work she builds (see Salvatori, 2000).

But of course, they might. And that possibility is another lesson to take home from the concept of the trading zone. You never know what will happen. The very divisions between the disciplines, which some find so disturbing, can be a resource of great value for the larger project of understanding and improving teaching and learning. Indeed, in Gallison's view, "It is the *disorder* of the scientific community—the laminated, finite, partially independent strata supporting one another; it is the *dis*unification of science—the intercalation of different patterns of argument—that is responsible for its strength and coherence" (1997, p. 844).

This point is worth underlining. The teaching commons is a space where people can have access to each other's work, but it is not a "commons" in the sense of being all the same, of sacrificing difference for homogeneity. Its vibrancy, like that of a city's, lies in the number, variety, and distinctiveness of its neighborhoods. Disciplinary neighborhoods are especially important to faculty who start looking more closely at learning, because the disciplines are the ports of both embarkation and arrival for their work. The questions that spark the work come from teaching biology or English or accounting or psychology—or even an interdisciplinary subject—to specific students in particular settings. And the lessons that flow from the work are meant to feed back to others engaged in teaching that field to other students in other settings. This is so, regardless of the scale of the effort, as long as it is made available in some way to peers. The scholarship of teaching and learning may involve modest efforts that faculty can fit into their academic lives with relative ease—for example, documenting and reflecting on teaching and learning in a single course. It may involve small-scale classroom inquiry. Or it may be part of a larger initiative, involving more formal research and evaluation designs, and perhaps collaboration with colleagues in other settings. For all these possibilities, the first audience—if not in fact, then in principle—remains one's disciplinary peers.

But the scholarship of teaching and learning is also an interdisciplinary enterprise, because no single field has all the questions, theories, or methods needed to illuminate student learning. Faculty involved in this work need access to venues where they can meet like-minded people from many disciplines—neighboring ones as well as those distant from their own. They need access to the teaching commons where they can share their wares, come home with other ideas, and use them to create something new. The literary critic Terry Eagleton has observed that "major art often flourishes on the fault lines between civilizations, fed by complex cross-currents between one form of life and another" (2004, p. 31). Judging from the experience of faculty who take up the scholarship of teaching and learning, the play between disciplinary cultures also stimulates pedagogical creativity.

The scholarship of teaching and learning is a powerful "development" experience precisely because it builds *on* and builds *up* the commitments that most faculty already have to their students and to their fields. Faculty who have bitten into the apple of pedagogy early in their educational lives as undergraduates or graduate students have an advantage here, because they enter their professional careers with some knowledge about the intellectual and collegial possibilities that heightened attention to teaching and learning can bring. But it is never too late to travel, explore—and return with stories to tell. As forums for this kind of work multiply, the scholarship of teaching and learning will become less risky, better known, and more rewarding.

In our work with educators on all kinds of campuses, in a full range of fields, we have heard (and shared) both cautions and hopes about the pathways that might take faculty into the scholarship of teaching and learning. "The scholarship of teaching and learning is not the kind of thing that should be required of all," one scholar told us, "but I want everyone to know something about it and to respect it" (Response to CASTL Scholars Survey, 2004). We would add that all faculty should have access to a map of the teaching commons (or at least of those regions closest to their own pedagogical concerns). They should also have support for visiting the commons when the need arises, appropriate recognition when they use what they find to improve their students' learning, and appropriate rewards for making their work public and giving back to the commons.

NOTES

1. This epigraph is from Spencer Benson's personal introduction to his fellow CASTL Scholars on the CASTL listserv, April 16, 2001 (Benson, 2001b).

Benson is an associate professor in the Department of Cell Biology and Molecular Genetics, and director of the Center for Teaching Excellence at the University of Maryland-College Park. His many accomplishments in science education include chairing the American Society of Microbiology's Board of Education's Undergraduate Education Committee and the ASM's teaching division. The Carnegie Foundation and the Council for the Advancement and Support of Education named Benson 2002 Maryland Professor of the Year, and he is also the recipient of a 2003 University of Maryland System Regents Teaching Award.

2. There is a huge literature on the relationship between teaching and research. See the insightful analysis of this genre of research by Hattie and Marsh (1996), who conclude: "Institutions need to reward creativity, commitment, investigativeness, and critical analysis in teaching and research and particularly value these attributes when they occur in both teaching and research" (p. 534). Scholars in the U.K. and Australia have been particularly interested in the nexus between teaching and research. See, for example, recent work by Angela Brew (2001, 2003), Lewis Elton (2001), and Alan Jenkins (Jenkins and Associates, 1998, 2002).
3. Historian Lendol Calder (Response to CASTL Scholars Survey, 2004) summed up beautifully that exhilarating but disturbing sense that some scholars of teaching and learning feel at having entered a new world they had not seen before:

   As a new professor, drunk on the high spirits distilled from positive course evaluations, I rested easily in the knowledge, or what passed for knowledge, that I was a "great," "superb," "wonderful" teacher. But I'm younger than that now. Many are the days I walk to class thinking that, by the standards of the scholarship of teaching and learning, the teaching I'm bringing that day is poorly designed for deep understanding. Even after all the work I've done in the area of assessment, it's downright depressing to know how little I know about my students and what they are learning. Meanwhile, the work I put into courses remains constant, instead of abating as with colleagues who finished writing lectures years ago and have turned to other interests. . . . Still, no question about it: I'd rather live discerningly with the scholarship of teaching and learning than happily without it, but deceived.

4. This section draws from *Balancing Acts,* Huber's 2004 study of the scholarship of teaching and learning in academic careers.
5. This is a lesson we have learned from Brian Coppola. See, for example, his description of structured study groups in undergraduate chemistry

(Coppola, Daniels, and Pontrello, 2001) as well as the chapters on Coppola's own career in *Balancing Acts: The Scholarship of Teaching and Learning in Academic Careers* (Huber, 2004).

6. Mastery learning is an approach to teaching and learning based on the idea that different students can learn the same material in different amounts of time. John Carroll (1963) and Benjamin Bloom (1981) are widely associated with developing this approach for schoolchildren. Bernstein's route to mastery learning was through the work of Columbia University behavioral psychologist Fred Keller (1968), whose "personalized system of instruction," involving a course design that allowed students to move through units of instruction at their own pace, gained followers in higher education. For an account of Bernstein's "Keller Plan" teaching, see Huber, 2004.
7. "Start where the students are" is a point often made in literature about teaching, drawing from learning theory (see Bransford, Brown, and Cocking, 1999). But anthropologist Susan Wright, former director of the U.K.'s Subject Network for Sociology, Anthropology, and Political Science, arrives at a similar destination by a different route. In seeking an appropriate stance for faculty development in the fields of sociology, anthropology, and politics, Wright argues the point by citing lessons from these fields' own critiques of the organization of the welfare state in the United Kingdom in the 1970s, ideas of "positioned politics" developed in the 1980s, and their reconceptualizations of such concepts as "service" and "expertise" in the context of social and community work both at home and abroad (2003, pp. 1–5).
8. A new Center for the Advancement of Engineering Education was established with a five-year grant from the NSF in 2003 to "address critical national needs to advance scholarship in engineering teaching and learning, increase the use of effective pedagogies in engineering classrooms, and strengthen research and leadership skills of the engineering faculty and graduate student community" (Center for the Advancement of Engineering Education, n.d.).
9. In his article, "The Very Idea of Pedagogy," John Guillory reminds his English literature colleagues that "close reading" and indeed, "much of what constitutes criticism in the 20th century, emerged out of contexts in which the teaching of literature was precisely the object or issue in question" (2002, p. 167). According to the *New Princeton Encyclopedia of Poetry and Poetics,* John Crowe Ransom's *The New Criticism* (1941) introduced the term New Criticism for an approach that emphasized a close reading of a text (rather than the study of such historical and contextual

factors as the author's "background, ambience, and sources") as key to determining its literary merit (Brooks and Brogan, 1993, p. 834). Although this perspective may have opened doors to criticism for many students, Gerald Graff, who has written extensively on the history of teaching literature in college and university classrooms, argues: "By treating the contexts of literature as an extrinsic affair, the New Criticism made it all the more unnecessary to worry about how those contexts might be organized institutionally. But without a context, the student's 'direct' experience of literature itself tends to result either in uncertainty or facile acquiescence in an interpretive routine" (1987, p. 11).

10. The development of such forums in ten fields (history, English, interdisciplinary studies, communication, management, sociology, psychology, mathematics, chemistry, and engineering) are discussed by contributors to *Disciplinary Styles in the Scholarship of Teaching and Learning* (Huber and Morreale, 2002a). This is a fast-moving area, however, so some of the forums mentioned here were established after these essays were written.
11. This section draws on discussions of interdisciplinary exchange in the scholarship of teaching and learning in Huber (2000) and Huber and Morreale (2002b).
12. For a discussion of these issues see, for example, the American Association for Higher Education's series on service learning in the disciplines, edited by Edward Zlotkowski.

5

THE CAMPUS AS COMMONS

Our experience has also taught us that one initiative in an institution creates ripple effects in other parts of the institution, effecting systemic change. As a result of our campus conversations, we are moving toward a clearer understanding of the scholarship of teaching and learning; this understanding is beginning to convert catchphrases like "the importance of teaching" and "teaching institution" from vague slogans into affirmations of the value of teaching and learning as institutional priorities.[1]

METAPHORS OPEN WINDOWS on all manner of things, and higher education is no exception. When campuses are compared to battleships or ocean liners, for instance—as they often are—attention is focused on the slow (some would say *stubbornly* slow) pace of change. "Universities in the past have been remarkable for their historic continuity," write the authors of a 1980 Carnegie Council report, "and we may expect this same characteristic in the future. They have experienced wars, revolutions, depressions, and industrial transformations, and have come out less changed than almost any other segment of their societies" (Carnegie Council on Policy Studies in Higher Education, 1980, p. 9). But metaphors conceal as well as reveal, and the image of a slow, oceangoing behemoth may hide the fact that colleges and universities *are* changing. In this chapter, our aim is to ask how the scholarship of teaching and learning is altering work and life on campus.

The answer depends, of course, on where you look and whom you ask. Some campuses have been quick to embrace the scholarship of teaching and learning, others slower, more skeptical. In some settings the idea has met with broad acceptance and enthusiasm; in others (and not always the ones you might expect), the language itself has been impossible to use, or a source of conflict.[2] We think of a quip made about teaching portfolios when they were new, as a "technology yet to be invented for a culture that . . . doesn't yet exist" (Edgerton, Hutchings, and Quinlan, 1991, p. 6). No doubt some observers on some campuses today would make a similar assessment of the scholarship of teaching and learning.

It is notable, though, that since 1998 when the CASTL program was first announced in the newsletter of our partner organization, the American Association for Higher Education, some two hundred campuses have answered the call, making a commitment to grapple with definitions, analyze local impediments and opportunities, and undertake some kind of initiative to bring the scholarship of teaching and learning into the institutional mainstream. And in a significant number of settings the work has taken hold in important ways. Today we see institutions of higher education—as leaders on one of the campuses put it—"orienteering their way back to their central mission: teaching and learning" (Albert, Moore, and Mincey, 2004, p. 191). Naturally, the details of this journey vary from campus to campus (not to mention from person to person on the *same* campus). Relevant developments are not always tied explicitly to, or undertaken in the name of, the scholarship of teaching and learning; nor are they fully aligned and consistent. There are counterforces at work and plenty of mixed signals. Even so, the general contours of the shift are evident in the growing number and size of communities on campus in which pedagogical work is talked about, exchanged, and built on; in new structures to support scholarly work on teaching and learning; and in emergent policies that create incentives and rewards for such work—three developments we trace in this chapter. As we will argue, colleges and universities today are increasingly connecting with the larger teaching commons.

Expanding Campus Conversations

Writing in *Change* magazine, Parker Palmer once proposed that the improvement of teaching and learning calls for a "movement theory of change" (1992). His point was to emphasize the critical role of individual energies, passions, discontents, and purpose in changing the status quo. That dynamic is central to the scholarship of teaching and learning. As we learned in our survey of CASTL Scholars, 94 percent became involved in the work "in order to find new colleagues" (Cox, Huber, and Hutchings, 2004). This is a key motif in the work on many campuses, where attention to teaching and learning has entailed, as Eugene Rice puts it, a move from "my work" to "our work" (1995). On many campuses, that is, the scholarship of teaching and learning is an antidote to the much-invoked "pedagogical solitude" diagnosed by Lee Shulman (1993, p. 6).

Often, this move toward "our work" occurs most readily, at least at first, outside of departmental boundaries, perhaps around a crosscutting theme or practice. At Middlesex Community College (Massachusetts), for instance, it was a small group of faculty from several different fields who set the scholarship of teaching and learning in motion by discovering a shared concern about their students' low motivation for academic work—a topic, in the words of the campus provost at the time, that "evokes in faculty the same feelings often associated with a grief reaction: anger, denial, depression, perhaps acceptance—and certainly much wringing of hands" (Sperling, 2003, p. 597). Faculty formed a study group committed to reading the research literature on motivation and undertaking modest interventions and investigations in their own classrooms. Their small circle eventually generated a larger community of practice whose work continues to grow and evolve as "charter members now serve as mentors to the newer members" (Gleason and Klein, 2004, p. 78).

Similar dynamics can be seen in other settings and contexts. Many faculty have found new colleagues and new directions for their teaching and scholarship through participation in cross-disciplinary curricular initiatives such as learning communities or writing across the curriculum. Pedagogies such as problem-based learning, and the use of simulations and cases, have brought groups together on some campuses. Service learning, undergraduate research, collaborative learning . . . all of these and more have been the basis for new forums and communities of exchange and study among faculty across departments. In addition, the assessment of student learning has been a focus for conversation. The Harvard Assessment Seminars, for instance—set in motion by then-president Derek Bok—brought together faculty, staff, and administrators, along with colleagues from several nearby institutions, to frame questions about their students' experience (How much do Harvard students really write, and how well? What kinds of feedback do they find most helpful?), study those questions, and share findings and recommendations with the larger campus community (Light, 1990, 1992, 2001). Because initiatives like these sometimes come with extramural funding that requires some form of reporting and evaluation (Harvard's effort had early support from the Fund for the Improvement of Postsecondary Education), such efforts have often been sites of inquiry and documentation, as well, inviting participants to turn their scholarly skills and habits on the processes and products of their own educational reform efforts.

Technology looms especially large in this story. Whether through small pockets of activity among early adopters who find one another in far-flung corners of the campus, or through top-down initiatives that bring together larger numbers of faculty, technology has been a magnet, bringing together colleagues who are eager to trade insights from innovations in their own classrooms. As one participant in such work puts it, "Technology is a force for disruption, calling everything pedagogical into question and opening up practices for scrutiny" (Ottenhoff, 2004; see also Christensen, 2003, and Christensen and Raynor, 2003). On many campuses, faculty who share these interests find one another and work together across a wide range of disciplines and fields to ask and explore questions about the impact of technology's "disruptions" of student learning—questions that matter both to professors using such technology and to administrators who foot the bill.

Organizing inquiry and exchange around student learning has also catalyzed important developments *within* departments—though, as those in academe know (this must seem odd to outsiders), the department is often a greater challenge than cross-disciplinary contexts when it comes to a focus on pedagogy. A case study of Stanford University, for instance, shows that interdisciplinary programs are more likely to undertake significant educational reform, whereas departments remain resistant (Cuban, 1999). As one CASTL participant put it, "There is a particularly strong lack of support at the departmental level. A small minority of chairs participate in scholarship of teaching and learning activities or encourage their faculty to do so" (Darden, Response to CASTL Scholars Survey, 2004). And yet a number of developments in departments show what is possible.

Seemingly modest changes can, for instance, make a real difference. In the early 1990s at the University of Nebraska-Lincoln, faculty in the psychology department pioneered what they called a "teaching circle," a term that has spread and come to mean "a variety of arrangements through which a small group of faculty members makes a commitment to work together over a period of at least a semester to address questions and concerns about their teaching and their students' learning" (Hutchings, 1996, p. 7). The idea, quite simply, is to provide a sustained forum for discussion and exchange about teaching where none exists. In some departments, participation in teaching circles has been taken into account in annual reviews (Bernstein, 1996), but the rewards are intrinsic as well. One teaching circle participant from Kent State University explained: "This hasn't been a department where people throw chairs at each other or anything, but our teaching circles have certainly fostered greater collegiality. They've put important teaching topics on the table and changed the way people relate to one another. The dialogue about teaching has really started" (Jameson, 1996, p. 9).

A variation on the departmental teaching circle is now taking shape in the history department at Gustavus Adolphus College, catalyzed by Sam Wineburg's prizewinning volume *Historical Thinking and Other Unnatural Acts* (2001). Captivated by Wineburg's study of the relationship between how professional historians think about and teach their field and the ways of thinking about the past that students bring to the classroom, the chair saw "a perfect opportunity for our department" (G. Kaster, e-mail to the authors, September 26, 2004). In no time at all, copies of the book were in the hands of every department member, grist for a year of discussion and inquiry (supported by a campus faculty-development program funded by the Bush Foundation) about ways to foster "among more of our students the kind of deep and 'unnatural' historical thinking Wineburg pinpoints" (Kaster, 2004, p. 2). Indeed, history majors are also reading the book, making students active participants in the project. Over time, the effort is aimed at producing, using, and learning from a set of "exercises," modeled on those used by Wineburg, to gather information about students' historical thinking. Such work not only raises the level of pedagogical discourse in the department ("formal conversation about teaching, learning, and thinking historically has been all too rare," the chair confesses) but promises to produce tools and insights that can be used beyond the department as well.

At the University of Michigan, the mathematics department has become a site for a similar kind of inquiry. The Mathematics Teaching Seminar, now in its third year, is a collaboration of faculty and graduate students from both mathematics and education, led by a former mathematics department chair, a past president of the American Mathematical Society, and a professor of mathematics education. It started by asking, "What do we want, and expect, our students to learn, and be like mathematically, after emerging from our first-year courses?" The mathematicians proposed an admirably lofty portrait. Next question: "How can we *know* what these students are actually like mathematically?" Here the educators offered help; a structured interview was collectively designed to explore student understanding of the derivative, as a concept and tool. It started with questions like, "Your younger brother asks you, 'What is this thing called the derivative?' How would you respond?" And later, more formally, "What is the definition of the derivative of $f(x)$ at $x = a$?" Several hourlong interviews were videotaped, and studied by the seminar. They both startled and fascinated the mathematicians, who had had little experience deeply probing students' mathematical thinking. And there was surprising lack of consensus about how to evaluate its quality (H. Bass, e-mail to the authors, October 24, 2004). These, and related explorations of how students might learn to "think like a mathematician" are reminiscent of the work of Curt Bennett and Jackie Dewar, described in Chapter Three.

One final example: several departments at the University of Wisconsin-La Crosse have been pursuing the scholarship of teaching and learning through *lesson study,* a process in which faculty jointly develop, teach, observe, analyze, and revise lessons for their courses.[3] "Every step in the process has been a surprise in some way," notes William Cerbin, who directs the project in the four participating disciplines of English, biology, psychology, and economics. The lesson turns out to be a particularly useful unit of analysis, in part because it offers a modest, doable way for faculty to begin the kind of inquiry entailed in the scholarship of teaching and learning, but also, Cerbin explains, because it opens a window on larger issues related to goals for student learning. The psychology group, for instance, "discussed the importance of linking the lesson to larger goals of the course . . . and one of the biologists talked about how this opened up broader discussions about the goals for their majors" (William Cerbin, e-mail to the authors, September 30, 2004). The work of each department team is documented in an annotated video of the lesson, lesson materials, and a research lesson report that describes the lesson, analyzes student performance, and explains what the instructors learned.

What we see in these examples, whether in or across disciplines, is at least the beginning of what might be called the *campus as commons,* with communities of thought and practice growing up around matters pedagogical. The particular shape and character of these communities must, of course, respond to needs and opportunities that themselves evolve over time. Teaching circles, assessment seminars, book groups, lesson study . . . these are initiatives that have beginnings and ends, though one may well lead to another (see Table 5.1).

Our point is not that any one of these approaches is the right one but that the character of conversation about pedagogy has begun to shift. Whereas in the past talk about teaching and learning has, on many campuses, been a pretty informal business, taking place primarily in hallways and staircases, one now also finds more organized, purposeful occasions for such exchange. Indeed, over the past several years it has been possible to map significant growth in forums for conversation about teaching and learning, many of which are campus-based. "What has been surpris-

Table 5.1. Sources of Support That Advance Involvement in the Scholarship of Teaching and Learning

	Percent of Respondents			
	Not Present	Present but Unimportant to My Work	Present and Somewhat Important to My Work	Present and Very Important to My Work
Supportive attitudes of departmental colleagues.	25	17	36	18
Release time from regular duties.	57	5	13	23
Campus funding for projects focused on teaching and learning.	35	17	29	19
Tenure and promotion policies that encourage the scholarship of teaching and learning.	54	20	20	6
Professional development activities at my campus that focus on the scholarship of teaching and learning.	17	18	39	24

Source: *Cox, Huber, and Hutchings, CASTL Scholars Survey, 2004.*

ing," observes a Carnegie study of this development, "is not only how *many* forums there are right now for this exchange, but how *surprised* people seem to be to find this out. In other words, what we are finding appears to be at odds with the prevailing stereotype that there has been little investment of intellectual interest and energy in teaching and learning in higher education" (Huber, 1999).

Making a Place for Good Work

Communities of conversation about teaching and learning often depend largely on the intrinsic motivation of participants, leveraged sometimes (less and less as budgets shrink) by a box lunch or wine and cheese. But if the scholarship of teaching and learning is to have a durable presence and impact on campus, it must be nourished with heartier fare. Friends and friendly exchange are necessary but not sufficient. To put the point a little differently, the scholarship of teaching and learning must move from personal engagement by small numbers of people to more structural arrangements.

One such manifestation is the campus-based center for teaching and learning. These centers have a significant history, and clearly predate the current phenomenon and language of the scholarship of teaching and learning. One of the earliest was the Center for Research on Learning and Teaching at the University of Michigan, founded in 1962, a model for a first real wave of centers developed in the 1970s and early 1980s with support from foundations committed to instructional enhancement (Quinlan, 1991). A recent survey by the Professional and Organizational Development Network—the association to which many faculty developers belong—suggests that the number of such centers is on the rise. "Many more institutions are starting faculty development programs than are closing them," reports POD president Dee Fink (2004, p. 1). This is certainly our impression as well.[4] Carnegie regularly hears about the establishment of a new center; recently, for instance, the director of a new center at Dartmouth College visited the foundation to talk with us about his plans and how they might connect with larger developments.

The growth in teaching centers is not surprising. They serve as sanctuaries for faculty eager to find colleagues with whom they can trade their pedagogical wares. They are clearinghouses for practical resources and research on teaching and learning, and help connect faculty with wider networks of innovation beyond the campus by bringing in consultants and speakers, for instance. Often they provide small grants for trying out new classroom approaches, or for travel to a conference where pedagogical work can be shared with others. And, on many campuses, teaching centers are an important crossroads where multiple initiatives intersect and can be coordinated in ways that add value for the institution.

Moreover, many of these centers have explicitly embraced the principles behind the scholarship of teaching and learning, promoting public discussion of pedagogical work, providing a home for faculty engaged in it, and moving toward more evidence- and inquiry-based approaches to the improvement of teaching and learning.[5] At the University of Wyoming, for instance, guidelines for teaching-innovation grants require that faculty not only do something new in their classroom but also gather evidence about the impact of their new approach. The Wyoming center also sponsors an "invisible college" to nurture scholars of teaching and learning, who share their work with the rest of the campus community at brown bag sessions and campuswide colloquia.[6] At Notre Dame, the teaching center sponsored a group of faculty interested in posing questions about their students' learning, designing a study to pursue those questions, and sharing results with campus colleagues and beyond. Some centers publish journals, online newsletters, and even edited collections featuring the work of local scholars of teaching and learning. Wyoming's center for teaching developed a collection of essays entitled *Warming Up the Chill* (Milford, Nelson, and Kleinsasser, 2003), featuring work identified by students as important to the climate for learning in the classroom. At Western Carolina University, the teaching center sponsors an online journal for the scholarship of teaching and learning called *Mountain Rise,* which joins online outlets such as *Inventio* from George Mason University, and the *Journal of the Scholarship of Teaching and Learning* from Indiana University. Many such journals are peer-reviewed and attract both writers and readers from a broad, even international, community.

Of course, not every campus has a teaching center, and in some settings the center may *not* be the place to locate the scholarship of teaching and learning, either because the center has other priorities or because it does not have the trust of the faculty.[7] Thus, some campuses have invented new structures, independent from existing, more broad-based units. Michigan State, for instance, now has a Center for the Scholarship of Teaching and Learning. The University of Georgia has established a Teaching Academy, a "freestanding, faculty-organized, and faculty-driven" community committed to pedagogical scholarship (Broder and Kalivoda, 2004, p. 33). Whatever the language, and whether newly established or long-standing, structures to promote serious work on teaching and learning are being developed on more and more campuses. A 2002 study of campuses involved in the CASTL program revealed that 61 percent had developed new structures to support such work (Babb, 2003).

Along with new structures comes a new philosophy. Rather than "emergency rooms for faculty in pedagogic arrest" (Shulman, 2004c, p. 213), the structures emerging on campus today are increasingly dedicated to inquiry, evidence, documentation, knowledge building, and exchange. Reports from campuses participating in CASTL indicate a shift from "a deficit model" of teaching improvement (Randall, 2004, p. 183) to one that builds on faculty's sense of what it means to understand their discipline or interdiscipline and to bring novice learners to deeper understandings. "The scholarship of teaching and learning perspective, which has challenged us to redefine the value of teaching improvement in terms of its effects on student learning, is gradually becoming the lingua franca of professional development," one campus reports (Ciccone, 2004, p. 49). Having a place to call home—a physical embodiment of the teaching commons—is an important step in the evolution of this common language.

Campus Reward Systems

More and more faculty are seeking out campus communities of lively, substantive exchange about teaching and learning. New institutional structures are being created to facilitate, host, organize, and tap into these discussions. People who care about this work agree that these are important developments. But they want to see more. Indeed, in our visits to campuses, and in conference and workshop settings focused on the scholarship of teaching and learning, it is the question of promotion and tenure that is most on people's minds. What inroads, they ask us, have been made in this important arena of campus policy and practice? Will the scholarship of teaching and learning count in the reward system?[8]

Looking at the question historically, we see reasons to be hopeful. In 1994, seeking to learn about changes prompted by its report *Scholarship Reconsidered* (Boyer, 1990), the Carnegie Foundation surveyed chief academic officers at all four-year colleges and universities in the United States. Some 80 percent of responding provosts reported that their institutions either had recently reexamined their systems of faculty roles and rewards or planned to do so, and the most widely embraced goal of these reviews was to redefine such traditional faculty roles as teaching, research, and service (Glassick, Huber, and Maeroff, 1997). During those same years, hundreds of campuses sent participants to an annual national Forum on Faculty Roles and Rewards (FFRR) organized by the American Association for Higher Education. Eugene Rice, director of the FFRR, observed, "New issues related to the changing priorities, rewards, and responsibilities of the professoriate are drawn to our attention almost daily. Hundreds of campus projects designed to address these issues are now in place and examples of good practice are readily available" (Rice, 1995, p. 1). Many campuses began requiring more substantial evidence of teaching effectiveness, including not only student ratings but also evidence and artifacts that are peer-reviewed. Many turned to teaching or course portfolios focused on student learning. Among institutions that had made changes in their systems of faculty roles and rewards, 69 percent reported new methods for the evaluation of teaching (Glassick, Huber, and Maeroff, 1997).

A follow-up survey in 2002 conducted by the American Association for Higher Education updates the picture. As many as two-thirds of America's four year colleges and universities have not only reexamined faculty roles and rewards over the last decade (1991 to 2001) but "reported that their institution had changed mission and planning documents, amended faculty evaluation criteria, provided incentive grants, or developed flexible workload programs to encourage and reward a broader definition of scholarship" (O'Meara, 2005, p. 261). Among all chief academic officers, 35 percent report that teaching counts more than it did ten years ago, and only 2 percent report that it counts less than ten years ago. Similarly, among fifty-eight campuses completing a self-study for CASTL, 60 percent reported new policies that give a clearer place to the scholarship of teaching and learning in promotion and tenure decisions (Babb, 2003).[9] In short, there have been broad shifts at the level of campus policy when it comes to the status and rewards attached to the scholarship of teaching and learning.

Closer to the ground, it is clear too that policy changes can make a real and positive difference. As we write, faculty at the University of Notre Dame are considering a new plan for evaluating teaching performance that continues to examine student evaluations for each course, but adds an in-depth evaluation of a few representative courses taught by the faculty member in the last three years. Faculty peers will examine the vision for and overall design of each of the selected courses, the sculpting of the course environment, artifacts of student learning, and student satisfaction with their educational experience in those courses. Whether or not this plan is ultimately approved, it may well be pointing to the future at many institutions in the United States, where the very methods used to evaluate teaching will actually promote a scholarly approach to practice and improvement (Hutchings, 1996).

Things may become more problematic, however, when faculty engagements with teaching intensify, requiring larger investments of time, money, and intellectual resources. What about those whose interests and inquiries lead them beyond the "regular" work of teaching and learning to more extended pedagogical projects? What about those who are presenting their work at conferences, organizing sessions, leading initiatives, publishing papers, and further participating in the scholarly life of national teaching and learning communities, as well as those on their campuses or in their fields? These are the people most likely to face questions from colleagues about the wisdom of their scholarly commitments, and, if they are not yet tenured or promoted, they are also the most likely to face challenges to the normal progress of their careers.

It is this issue—the evaluation of one's scholarly choices and commitments by colleagues—that is the most troublesome for faculty who intensify their work on teaching and learning at earlier stages in their professional lives. To be sure, there will still be many whose scholarship of teaching and learning is a good fit in their institution. For example, Jose Feito at Saint Mary's College of California reports that his inquiries into the nature of intellectual community in the seminar were welcomed by colleagues as a kind of research that fit well both with the campus's mission and with his field, social psychology. But others have faced static, even at institutions where one would think such work would be welcome. One CASTL Scholar was initially turned down for tenure at his community college because he seemed too interested in *scholarship*: "We're here to teach," they told him. "We're not here to *think* about teaching. You should find yourself a job at a four-year school where you have time to think about teaching."

Indeed, professors risking new forms of scholarship *are* sometimes disappointed when it is time for a tenure, promotion, or merit review, and careers have been derailed. At the same time, stories of faculty who have been rewarded for their scholarly work on teaching and learning are now easier to find, and they hold important lessons. *Balancing Acts: The Scholarship of Teaching and Learning in Academic Careers* (Huber, 2004) documents the professional advancement of four research university faculty who have achieved national prominence for the scholarship of teaching and learning in their fields. Each was warned by caring and responsible mentors that they were taking risks in treating teaching so seriously. But all four persisted, found ways to make a persuasive case for their work in their own discipline and campus context, and were tenured and promoted. Their stories now circulate in their scholarly communities and on their campuses as signs that the scholarship of teaching and learning can be woven successfully into an academic career. That is the good news.

But even where the stories end happily, it is clear that there is a struggle. In part, this is because using the scholarship of teaching and learning for purposes of academic advancement is so new. Faculty attempting to make a case for such work may find that the "standard metrics"—despite their apparent objectivity—can make unfamiliar kinds of scholarship look substandard instead. The conferences and journals in which they present their work may not be well-known to departmental colleagues. The funding may be less generous, the external reviewers less prestigious; the methods might seem soft. Pedagogical and curricular reform projects are often highly collaborative, aimed at improving practice. They may also draw on literature from other fields, and involve unusual products, like course portfolios or new media materials. Perhaps most troubling is that successful teaching innovations often circulate without the innovator's name attached—making it hard to trace and lay claim to the impact of one's work.

This is not just another case in the teaching-versus-research debate. Faculty who bring their disciplinary expertise to community development have also had white-knuckle experiences gaining academic recognition for their work. In many fields, research itself is changing to include more multidisciplinary, collaborative work oriented to solving real-world problems, but decision making on the ground continues to reward most readily work that conforms to older norms. In short, many campuses have changed their promotion and tenure guidelines to encourage innovation, but whether this new work will *really* count is a question that is now being answered case by case (see Huber and Cox, 2004; Huber, 2004).

Case by Case and Boat by Boat

Indeed, the case-by-case nature of change on campus makes it hard to give a definitive account of the progress of the scholarship of teaching and learning. The metaphor of campus-as-battleship conveys an image of change as monolithic, unitary, and linear (not to mention slow), but in fact campuses are complex, living organisms where new developments occur in fits and starts, energetically in one quarter, sluggishly in another. Change is happening all the time, all over the place, but not in a neat, coordinated way, as if in response to a signal from the wheelhouse (if that's what the steering station on a large ship is called). It is messy in other ways as well. Policy related to promotion and tenure is often cited as the acid test—the aspect of campus life in which *real* change would need to be embodied—but the official language about such matters leaves lots of gray area up for grabs, and lots of translation to be done at various levels of the process. Moreover, promotion and tenure are only one relevant policy area. What happens at the point of hire, the process for annual review, posttenure review, teaching awards . . . all of these are moments that send signals (or not) about renewed and strengthened attention to teaching. And, of course, campus policy is only one factor in the decisions faculty make about how to spend scarce time. A notoriously independent breed, scholars follow their own passions, their own curiosities and priorities.

In his study of the history of teaching and learning at Stanford University, Larry Cuban documents the many obstacles to lasting structural reforms. But he says something very interesting. His account is not, he says, "a case of failed change." Rather, it reveals that "a complex institution can be both stable and change-prone simultaneously." And what he recommends as a route to more lasting forms of change is what he calls "*strategic* incrementalism or short-term tinkering toward a defined long-term purpose of redesigning university structures, processes, and cultures." In contrast to the often-invoked image of systemic reform as carefully coordinated and unitary, he sees the key to change in "a series of small but high-profile improvements aimed at a common purpose" (Cuban, 1999, pp. 199, 204).

This strikes us as an excellent description of campus developments related to the scholarship of teaching and learning. Rather than thinking of higher education as a battleship, it may make more sense to imagine a fleet of small boats. They don't all head in exactly the same direction, but increasingly there is a sense of convergence, of being part of something larger, of rowing toward some common destination—like the teaching commons. Progress like this is slow going, and not without puzzles of its own (the next chapter takes up some of the fundamental epistemological puzzles, for example), but the scholarship of teaching and learning on campus is clearly much more than a phrase today. Indeed, it may be that it will have arrived, hardwired and deeply embedded, only when the language starts to disappear and its habits, structures, policies, and practices come to be seen as simply "the way it is"—a given, and a reality we take for granted.

NOTES

1. This epigraph is from "An Ongoing Journey," by Lawrence S. Albert, Michael R. Moore, and Kathryn C. Mincey (2004). The quote appears on page 192, where the authors are describing the impact of the scholarship of teaching and learning (and participation in the CASTL program) on their campus, Morehead State University, in Morehead, Kentucky.
2. Especially in the early days of CASTL's work, we heard faculty, administrators, and leaders of disciplinary associations say that, although they embraced the ideas of the scholarship of teaching and learning, the language was off-putting to them or their colleagues; alternative vocabularies were needed for the campus to move ahead with the agenda.
3. Lesson study has become known to American educators primarily through its use in Japan, where it is a familiar routine through which teachers work together to hone lessons. William Cerbin, director of the lesson study project at the University of Wisconsin-La Crosse, recommends the video "Can You Lift 100kg?" (available from http://www.lessonresearch.net/), which depicts the process in an elementary science class in Japan. "Even though

the contexts of American colleges and universities differ," Cerbin says, "we have found this video both inspiring and illuminating" (William Cerbin, e-mail to the authors, September 30, 2004). The entire process, as well as a tutorial, is accessible on a multimedia Web site (see http://www.uwlax.edu/sotl/lsp) developed as part of the University of Wisconsin system's initiative on the scholarship of teaching and learning.

4. In 1994, 28 percent of four-year campuses reported having such a center (Glassick, Huber, and Maeroff, 1997). But it turns out to be difficult to get reliable figures about the number and growth of teaching and learning centers since then. One obstacle is definitional: smaller campuses and two-year institutions may not have "a center" in the sense of a physical space and separate staff, though they may have leadership and resources that serve the same purpose. Still, centers or centerlike functions are clearly on the rise. The Professional and Organizational Development Network notes a 20 percent increase in membership between 2001 and 2004 (Fink, 2004).
5. At the Peer Review of Teaching Project conference in April 2004 in Lincoln, Nebraska, Allison Pingree from Vanderbilt University presented a session on the implications of a more scholarly view of teaching for the work and role of teaching centers, highlighting a number of shifts: from work that is "remedial" to work that is inquiry-based and organized around questions, from work that is private to work that is shared and available for peer collaboration and review, from work that is focused on teaching methods to work that depends on evidence of student learning. Such shifts are not absolute, of course. One can focus on evidence of student learning and on teaching methods (and on the relationship between them). Nevertheless, as Pingree argued, the scholarship of teaching and learning may challenge teaching centers to rethink priorities and practices (Pingree, 2004).
6. The University of Wyoming has dubbed its scholarship of teaching and learning group "the inVISIBLE college," highlighting the agenda of going public while drawing on a longer history. The term was originally used to describe the group of scholars who later became the British Royal Society, founded in 1660 (see Nelson and Kleinsasser, 2004). Diane Crane's 1972 study, *Invisible Colleges,* explores how such social structures influence the development of ideas.
7. As Mills and Huber (2005) note, the growth of faculty development units in British universities has had a mixed reception among faculty members. "Whilst individual academics benefit from, and go on record as valuing their encounters with these units, those in the Humanities and Social Sciences seem to have a collectively negative perception of them. . . . In

the newer UK universities, where these centres promote disliked central government initiatives, educational development has become unpopular amongst academic staff skeptical of a growing managerialism" (p. 14).

8. This section draws on discussions of the scholarship of teaching and learning in faculty reward systems in Huber (2004) and Huber and Cox (2004).
9. Nationally, CASTL did an analysis of "Mapping Progress" reports completed by fifty-eight campuses active in the program in 2003. Of these, 95 percent reported having sponsored campuswide and departmental events, conferences, workshops, and retreats for faculty interested in the scholarship of teaching and learning, with regular increases in the percentage of faculty in attendance; 72 percent reported grants, stipends, or release time for faculty or departments for the scholarship of teaching and learning; and 71 percent reported new infrastructure, such as a teaching and learning center, office, committee, or positions. Sixty percent of campuses reported that the scholarship of teaching and learning was accepted in promotion and tenure decisions (see Babb, 2003).

6

KNOWLEDGE BUILDING AND EXCHANGE

An act of intelligence or of artistic creation becomes scholarship when it possesses at least three attributes: it becomes public; it becomes an object of critical review and evaluation by members of one's community; and members of one's community begin to use, build upon, and develop those acts of mind and creation.[1]

FACULTY WHO HAVE TAKEN UP the scholarship of teaching and learning offer ample, enthusiastic testimony of its power to change their own classrooms, to revitalize their teaching, and to improve their students' learning. Such changes are all to the good, and arguably the most important measure of the movement's impact. But by calling this work scholarship, we are also making a larger claim: that the scholarship of teaching and learning builds knowledge that others can use. What does this ambition entail, and what progress is being made toward meeting it?

For starters, Lee Shulman's call to make teaching *community property* (1993) has energized many experiments in making pedagogy public—a prerequisite for knowledge building and exchange. Scholars of teaching and learning present their work in conventional formats such as conference papers, published articles, and books. But they are also developing new modes of collaboration and sharing, like teaching circles and project groups, and new forms of presentation, like the course portfolio or the pedagogical colloquium, where a candidate for a job elaborates on his or her teaching philosophy and practice in a course that is important to the hiring department (Hutchings, 1996, 1998; Bernstein, 2001). In addition, electronic communications and repositories now make it much easier to consult colleagues about teaching problems, and to find resources that colleagues have developed in their own teaching, from syllabi to assignments, assessments, and learning materials, some with commentary and peer review.[2] Many scholars, too, are excited about the promise of electronic media for "publishing" rich representations of teaching and learning, including solutions to course design and classroom problems, and examples of student work (Hatch, Bass, Iiyoshi, and Pointer Mace, 2004). Understanding how the scholarship of teaching and learning contributes to knowledge means understanding the various forms and formats—traditional and cutting-edge—in which the work is represented.

But it is also important to see that the scholarship of teaching and learning, though it sometimes looks like more traditional forms of scholarship, has some of the distinctive characteristics of the newer modes of knowledge production found both within and outside academe: it is often collaborative and interdisciplinary, and always oriented to the improvement of practice (Gibbons and Associates, 1994; Nowotny, Scott, and Gibbons, 2001). And unlike pioneers of other emergent fields who have sought to establish new, separate disciplines, departments, or programs (see Gumport, 2002), scholars of teaching and learning are seeking to improve practice *within* the disciplines, departments, or programs where they already teach.[3] Indeed, as we have seen, many advocates of the scholarship of teaching and learning hope to infuse its animating ideas of questioning, exploring, trying out, and going public throughout the pedagogical life of their institutions.

Higher education is still a long way from that goal. The teaching commons is growing as more work becomes public in the sense of being available for use. But its vitality depends also on the scholarship of teaching and learning becoming public in a second sense—on whether, as Lee Shulman says in this chapter's epigraph, "members of [the] . . . community begin to use, build upon, and develop those acts of mind and creation" (1999, p. 15). Whether and how the scholarship of teaching and learning becomes a prominent part of higher education—influencing the way in which large numbers of faculty approach their work as teachers—will ultimately depend on whether it substantially enriches the commons by producing the kinds of knowledge that educators actually use to build more effectively on one another's work.

What Kinds of Knowledge Are Useful?

Faculty members have always built on each other's work as teachers. Yet with the important exception of commercially produced textbooks and teaching materials, this has most often involved informal modeling and advice from within the compass of a professor's personal ties. Most faculty have learned to teach by watching their own teachers; they gain new ideas for course design by sharing syllabi with close colleagues; they seek advice from each other privately, in corridors, offices, and over e-mail and the telephone. Much of what faculty know about teaching and learning has been gained more or less informally as practicing members of their own disciplinary communities, although some have had opportunities to learn from colleagues in neighboring fields—for example, through the design or teaching of interdisciplinary courses or programs, or through efforts sponsored by a teaching and learning center. And, of course, there has always been a pedagogical literature, which offers opportunities to learn from those farther away.

We can turn to the field of literary studies for an example of this familiar pattern at its best. Wayne Booth, a distinguished literary theorist from the University of Chicago, is a passionate advocate for undergraduate teaching. In *The Vocation of a Teacher* (1988), a collection of his speeches and essays, Booth offers a charming footnote on the sources of his knowledge about teaching that is probably diagnostic for the field as a whole. In that note (pp. 209–210), he first lists several books "that teach about teaching by force of example"—Ashton-Warner's *Teacher* (1963), Barzun's *Teacher in America* (1986 [1945]), Erskine's *My Life as a Teacher* (1948), Highet's *The Art of Teaching* (1950), Narayan's *The English Teacher* (1945), and Passmore's *The Philosophy of Teaching* (1980). On the more technical side he lists "Joe Axelrod's obscure little pamphlet on 'The Discussion Technique in the College Classroom' (or some such title), published sometime in the late forties and now, so far as my own shelves can tell me, lost to the world." (Not quite lost: see Axelrod, 1949.) But, Booth admits, "More important than any of these have been thousands of staff meetings and conversations with colleagues in America and England." And, he adds, "I am . . . not even beginning to list the many works that have influenced my thinking about [my subject] or about what I ought to teach" (p. 210).

We take this account as fairly typical for many faculty members, at least until quite recently—and not just in literary studies. It is characterized by a willingness to separate questions about content, about which one claims expert knowledge, from questions about teaching, about which one does not. There is the heightened importance of meetings and personal conversations where the wisdom of practice is exchanged.[4] And, finally, there are books: usually not scholarly studies based on a search for the most up-to-date developments, but works that one has found more or less by chance at critical moments in one's career. For Booth, who probably is better read in this area than many of his generation, the majority of books are classics that were published when he was a young academic, at a time when there were fewer resources available than today.[5]

The scholarship of teaching and learning will not, we suspect, replace any of the traditional ways in which faculty gain inspiration and ideas about teaching and learning, but it *will* enhance the quality of those ideas, increase their circulation, and broaden their range. Faculty who intentionally document their teaching in course portfolios, who ask hard questions about their goals for student learning, who engage in varieties of classroom research will have better advice for their colleagues in the hallways and more considered contributions to make in committees. If they make this work public through the Web or more conventional genres, its quality will be further enhanced through the process of refining the work for "prime time" and through the possibilities for peer commentary and review. Making it public will also increase the chance that insights and results will find a wider audience. And everyone, from the scholar who does the work to those who hear about it, will learn about the written works and Web resources that informed the inquiry as it proceeded.

But a second sense of making teaching public comes into play here. Most faculty learn about the commons and its resources only when they start asking questions about teaching and learning that "the literature" (whatever its form or medium) can help them formulate and resolve (see Cross, 1998). Our survey of CASTL Scholars supports this observation. When asked whether their involvement in the scholarship of teaching and learning had heightened their interest in reading research on teaching and learning, 96 percent either agreed or strongly agreed (Cox, Huber, and Hutchings, 2004). Clearly, when faculty start thinking about teaching as a site for scholarship, they seek out work that can help them to understand the dimensions of the problem they are working on or to devise appropriate modes of documentation and inquiry.

We can look to the experience of David Takacs and Gerald Shenk of California State University-Monterey Bay for an example of this move to the literature—and to the work of colleagues in other fields—once faculty start thinking this way. Takacs and Shenk, as readers will recall from Chapter Three, coteach a course in California history with a community service component. But, although they are both longtime activists themselves, they only began reading work on education for social justice when they became involved in the scholarship of teaching and learning. They cite bell hooks' *Teaching to Transgress* (1994) as influential in their innovations in the course, projects on social justice by several other scholars as broadening their view of what was possible for their students, and advice from colleagues experienced with focus groups and interviews as helpful in shaping methods they used to explore students' learning (David Takacs, e-mails to the authors, October 5 and November 2, 2004).

What is striking in this example is how different modes and genres of knowledge building mix and strengthen each other when faculty decide to mine and share their practice in more formal ways. People still draw on their own experience and that of close colleagues, but they are now also drawing on the expertise of new colleagues who are examining issues in their own fields and classrooms, and on published findings and reflections by those far away. Because of their inquiries and reflection, scholars of teaching and learning can get better ideas for their own practice from others who have made their classroom studies public through the media and forums now available.

But why and how is this kind of knowledge valuable to faculty? One answer is that the knowledge needed for teaching is often deeply contextual and tied closely to the details of classroom practice. It is true that higher education has been less troubled by the theory-practice gap than have primary and secondary education, no doubt because virtually all the attention in colleges and universities has been on content knowledge; faculty are expected to incorporate into their teaching the latest developments in their field. Now, however, with pedagogy moving to center stage, it is important that higher education learn from the K–12 experience. Although instructors at any level can benefit from basic research on teaching or learning, it would be a mistake, in higher education as it has been in the lower grades, to assume that findings from such research can be simply "applied" or "translated" to practice in any straightforward way (National Research Council, 2002, p. 154).

In fact, according to studies cited in the National Research Council's report *Scientific Research in Education* (2002), the "prevailing model of research implementation—moving from basic research to development to large-scale implementation of programs—is based on simplistic assumptions about the nature of education and education research" (p. 156). The authors cite a National Academy of Education report (1999) that argues for a perspective similar to the one we develop here: it makes more sense to "view research production and research understanding as part of the same process" (National Research Council, 2002, p. 156). In other words—and this goes to the very heart of the scholarship of teaching and learning—*doing it enables one to use it*. Practitioners must participate in the effort if it is to have real consequences in the classroom.

This is only in part a matter of focusing faculty attention on pedagogical problems and directing their attention to the resources available for thinking them through. There are also epistemological issues at play. Teaching and learning at the classroom level are both highly dependent on contextual factors, and faculty often find as much to learn from the situated experience of other faculty as from studies done with methodologies designed to minimize the influence of context on research results. An example from Chapter Three is relevant here. Faculty who adopted Mariolina Salvatori's difficulty paper were persuaded to do so not because she could prove its effectiveness across settings but because her account of its genesis and use in her *own* setting was so powerful and rich. Lee Shulman argues that it is, in fact, the details of particular cases that allow for generalizability, helping the user determine "What is this a case of? How similar are the circumstances under which this study was conducted to the situation to which I might wish to generalize its findings? Is this work relevant to me and my circumstances?" (2002a, p. vi).

To be sure, there are scholars—especially in science fields—who are unlikely to try new pedagogical approaches unless they have the kind of warrant that only large-scale, quasi-experimentally designed educational research can provide. But our experience with faculty in mathematics, engineering, and the sciences shows that they, too, are stimulated by smaller-scale explorations of what it means to help students think like practitioners in their particular fields, as in the work of Bennett and Dewar, or learn cooperatively in large classrooms, as in the work of Dennis Jacobs. Indeed, scholars of all disciplinary stripes have found tools for thought, inquiry, and action not only in theoretical and large-scale empirical studies but also in work conducted in and around a single classroom or course. Jose Feito's conception of intellectual community, based on close study of his own classroom, has, for instance, been a useful tool for others studying the pedagogy of the academic seminar (see, for example, Greene, 2004, and Gale, 2004). And though the quality of the data is certainly important in making his framework useful, its power also depends on the freshness of language (his notion of intellectual intimacy), the elegance of the framework, and the clarity with which he talks about the implications of his findings in his own classroom.

This is the kind of process envisioned by Barbara Walvoord when she observes that the use of the scholarship of teaching and learning "may resemble how a reader uses a biography or an autobiography. No one claims that the reader ought to be able to replicate the writer's life. Yet people read biographies and autobiographies and use them to guide their own lives and decisions" (2000, p. 2).[6] The scholarship of teaching and learning may inform practice, she concludes, not only by providing ideas for methods, materials, or assessment but also by inspiring, moving, and changing a teacher's perspective, attitude, or vision.

It is, in short, precisely the contextually rich nature of practitioner inquiry that makes the scholarship of teaching and learning so useful to faculty in higher education. When such work enters the teaching commons, faculty can see how others manage complexity in the classroom, and pose and address real-world problems in situations they know how to "read." They can identify a good question, a promising investigative strategy, an assignment or assessment design that they might try out or include in their own repertoire, and they are aided in incorporating it into their own work by their understanding of how the original context differs from their own.

Rich Representations

The importance of context in knowledge building around matters pedagogical brings with it a crucial corollary. Although there is a place for general principles and lists of best practices to guide improvement, also needed are representations of teaching and learning that capture more of the full act of teaching. Indeed, it is through such rich representations that the scholarship of teaching and learning will make its greatest contribution to the teaching commons—and those contributions cannot, then, be limited to conventional publication. Most faculty recognize that there is much about teaching practice that cannot be easily conveyed on paper, and there are now important experiments using new media that make it possible to represent teaching and learning in new ways.

The Massachusetts Institute of Technology's OpenCourseWare (OCW) project is a case in point. A large-scale Web-based electronic publishing initiative, the OCW "makes MIT's core teaching materials—lecture notes, problem sets, syllabi, reading lists, simulations, etc.—freely and openly available for noncommercial educational purposes" (MIT OpenCourseWare, 2004, p. 2). The project plans to publish all MIT courses (about nine hundred were online by fall 2004) and then to begin a cycle of updating. The project has not only enjoyed a lively response from educators, students, and self-learners from around the globe but has also helped MIT faculty themselves become more reflective about their own teaching and more aware of what their colleagues are doing in the classroom—benefits likely to be further enhanced as the project adds information about *how* the courses are taught.[7]

Many other experiments are under way. For example, the Peer Review of Teaching Project headquartered at the University of Nebraska, the Visible Knowledge Project based at Georgetown University, and the Carnegie Foundation's Knowledge Media Laboratory (KML) have all explored alternative or additional genres to enable scholars of teaching and learning to document their work online in ways not possible in regular talk or print. The Peer Review of Teaching Project developed Web-based course portfolios by faculty at five universities, using a format that is highly structured, relatively simple to create, but still somewhat "texty" (as technology people say)—thus connecting to the reading and writing habits of most academics (Bernstein, 2001).[8] The Knowledge Media Laboratory takes a different approach, developing elaborate electronic portfolios with a strategic mix of text, audio, and video, to establish a "library, laboratory, and museum" of teaching and learning that other faculty can study and learn from online. And the Visible Knowledge Project has adapted the KML's user-friendly "snapshot tool" to provide structured templates for making dynamic, visually appealing electronic posters of individual projects, as well as to facilitate the process and to represent the products of collaborative work.[9]

In fact, technology circles in higher education are buzzing with experiments in ways to help faculty and students make teaching and learning public, although it is much too early to know what will result. As we write, the brightest minds are working on tough questions about archiving, indexing, and charting the life cycles of such representations. Most important to the future of the teaching commons is whether and how these works are being used. If they build it, will you come? Will people actually enlarge their pedagogical imaginations through engaging with electronic portfolios, snapshots, and posters, and other online representations of teaching and learning? In other words, what will it take to build a "readership," "usership," or "audience" for these new kinds of work?

The Peer Review of Teaching Project, the Visible Knowledge Project, and the Knowledge Media Laboratory (as well as the CASTL program itself) have all addressed this need, first by creating a supportive, collaborative context for *doing* the scholarship of teaching and learning, and second by helping their participants produce work that will enter wider communities of practice. The KML encourages viewers of their gallery of online portfolios and snapshots to create similar galleries in their own institutions, to read the materials for ideas to improve their teaching, and to use the portfolios as "launching points for discussions and reflections, peer review of teaching and learning, collaborative inquiries, and further investigations" (see the KML Web site). As leaders of the KML and VKP explain: "The convergence of multimedia applications, Web-based tools, and networked information systems with the growth of a more complex vision of teaching can lead to two critical developments. . . . The first is the establishment of a broader, collaborative research paradigm, where a community of scholars might examine similar classroom phenomena and pool their evidence and findings. Second is the creation of a more flexible relationship between teaching processes, classroom inquiry, and published products" (Hatch, Bass, Iiyoshi, and Pointer Mace, 2004, p. 47).

Consider one provocative use of KML materials, where teacher educators are already engaging their students with the portfolio of Yvonne Divans Hutchinson, a teacher in the King-Drew Medical Magnet High School in Los Angeles (2003). The idea here is to foster what Lee Shulman calls a "triple play": (1) teachers create representations of critical aspects of teaching and learning in their K–12 classrooms; (2) teacher educators create representations of how they are using these resources in their college classrooms with teachers in training; and (3) student teachers create representations of their attempts to alter their own pedagogy in ways that are informed by the models they have studied. Another use is illustrated by the participants in VKP: nearly two-thirds said in a survey that reading others' online representations of their scholarship of teaching and learning was either "very effective" or "indispensable" to their own VKP projects (Randy Bass, e-mail to the authors, October 4, 2004). The Peer Review of Teaching Project has also attended to the use of its participants' portfolios. Indeed, one of the distinctive features of this initiative has been the effort to cultivate an informed readership—exploring what it actually feels like, on the one hand, to review portfolios by teachers one does not know, and, on the other, to have one's own portfolio read and reviewed by such readers.

It will be interesting to find out if portfolio writers become habitual portfolio readers, or if snapshot or poster writers become regular snapshot or poster readers. It is arguably the case that academics learn to read traditional scholarship in their fields by doing it and writing it as graduate students and later as professionals themselves. Why should the scholarship of teaching and learning be different? If, as KML director Toru Iiyoshi has suggested to us, writing in these new genres may be key to developing literacy in them, then the work of KML and VKP and other initiatives to create Web-based tools that faculty can use to document and share work assumes an even greater importance.

Questions of Quality

Questions about what kinds of knowledge, in what forms and formats, are useful for the advancement of teaching and learning are also, inevitably, questions about quality. Only good work can "inform other members of the community, engage them in deep and significant conversations, provide a basis for the formation of communities of scholars, and be evaluated in that community" (Shulman, 1998, p. 7). Busy academics are simply not going to venture far into this new territory unless they find something worthwhile there.

Questions of quality in the scholarship of teaching and learning are complicated, of course, by its different genres and disciplinary styles. As one can see from even a quick glance at the essays in *Disciplinary Styles in the Scholarship of Teaching and Learning* (Huber and Morreale, 2002a), chemists, psychologists, and sociologists, for example, are likely to have different expectations. Understandably, faculty will look at new work for the signs of serious intellectual engagement that characterize scholarship with which they are more familiar. Consider the criticism that one group of historians made of articles that offer a personal account of a clever solution to a classroom problem—until recently the most common type of published work on college-level teaching and learning in their field. Historians seldom take such articles seriously, they say, because such work typically provides little or no evidence of student learning, incorporates little convincing historical argument, and cites few references to previous work (Calder, Cutler, and Kelly, 2002; Calder, 2002).

The questions that educators have about quality in the scholarship of teaching and learning often revolve around epistemological issues implicit in practitioner research, and concern genres and methods that remain close to practice. As we have seen, the scholarship of teaching and learning takes a close look at a faculty member's approach to classroom problems, leaving much of the blooming, buzzing context intact. Consider course portfolios, which must juggle the competing goals of scope and granularity of representation, and of richness, visual appeal, and ease of use. The Peer Review of Teaching Project has encouraged faculty to produce short, carefully structured portfolios that can be easily read and reviewed by others, whereas the electronic course portfolios created by the Knowledge Media Laboratory have opted for greater elaboration and richness of representation so that readers can see what the pedagogy or learning in question actually looks like.

Classroom inquiry, too, operates within the constraints of particular settings, and, although it sometimes entails a quasi-experimental design (using one method with one section of a course and another with another), in some situations this is not practical or even ethical. Statistician John Holcomb, contemplating just such a design to test an approach he had developed for an introductory course, writes:

> One thing I realized was that a control group model was not going to be very tenable in my situation because the bottom line—the thing I wanted to analyze—was students' ability to do a data-analysis project, and I couldn't see how to compare the performance of the "treatment group" with performance in a traditionally taught statistics course where students are never taught or asked to do this kind of problem. This is partly a methodological problem; I would be comparing apples and oranges. But it also has an ethical dimension. I ran into this wall when I asked myself whether it would be ethical to require students from a traditional course to perform in a way that they had no preparation for. [2002, p. 20]

Regardless of what design they choose, however, most scholars of teaching and learning recognize that the classroom does not lend itself to the same control over variables as the lab, nor the same attention to sampling and representativeness that working with large numbers of subjects can provide.

These methodological and ethical issues can be serious problems for scholars of teaching and learning when they present their accomplishments to colleagues who are unfamiliar with work of this kind. Yet, following the logic of *Scholarship Assessed* (Glassick, Huber, and Maeroff, 1997), the Carnegie Foundation's follow-up to *Scholarship Reconsidered* (Boyer, 1990), the fact that the genres and methods of the scholarship of teaching and learning often differ from those of the scholarship of discovery is not an indictment of its quality, but instead the key. *Scholarship Assessed* proposes that all modes of scholarship can be judged according to the same formal standards: clear goals, adequate preparation, appropriate methods, significant results, effective presentation, and reflective critique (see Exhibit 6.1). But these general characteristics of quality are only meaningful if translated in ways that allow the work to be judged on its own terms.[10]

Scholarship Assessed suggests questions to guide this process of translation. For *goals,* the report asks: Are the project's basic purposes clearly stated? Are the objectives realistic and achievable? Does the work address important questions in the field? "Teaching," Shulman says, "begins with a vision of the possible or an experience of the problematic. The teacher

Exhibit 6.1. Summary of Standards

Clear goals:
Does the scholar state the basic purposes of his or her work clearly? Does the scholar define objectives that are realistic and achievable? Does the scholar identify important questions in the field?

Adequate preparation:
Does the scholar show an understanding of existing scholarship in the field? Does the scholar bring the necessary skills to his or her work? Does the scholar bring together the resources necessary to move the project forward?

Appropriate methods:
Does the scholar use methods appropriate to the goals? Does the scholar apply effectively the methods selected? Does the scholar modify procedures in response to changing circumstances?

Significant results:
Does the scholar achieve the goals? Does the scholar's work add consequentially to the field? Does the scholar's work open additional areas for further exploration?

Effective presentation:
Does the scholar use a suitable style and effective organization to present his or her work? Does the scholar use appropriate forums for communicating work to its intended audiences? Does the scholar present his or her message with clarity and integrity?

Reflective critique:
Does the scholar critically evaluate his or her own work? Does the scholar bring an appropriate breadth of evidence to his or her critique? Does the scholar use evaluation to improve the quality of future work?

Source: *Glassick, C. E., Huber, M. T., and Maeroff, G. I. Scholarship Assessed: Evaluation of the Professoriate. San Francisco: Jossey-Bass, 1997, p. 36, Exhibit 2.1.*

builds a general view of how instruction might be improved, and/or senses that current instruction is unacceptable or a problem in some fashion" (1998, p. 6). This is why the most basic move in the scholarship of teaching and learning is the capacity to transform a "teaching problem" into a "problematic" or "researchable question," as Randy Bass suggests (1999b, p. 1). As we have seen, it is the quality of the questions asked, more than anything else, that gives work done in one classroom the power to inform innovation elsewhere.

Adequate preparation is the second standard. Does the project show an understanding of existing scholarship in the field? Does the scholar bring to it the necessary skills? Has he or she brought together the resources necessary to move the project forward? These questions highlight a special challenge for the scholarship of teaching and learning because in many disciplines there are no established traditions of inquiry and analysis, no training, and few outlets or funding sources for this kind of work. Still, as we have seen, the teaching commons in higher education is rapidly growing, and today's scholars of teaching and learning can for the most part count on more resources and support to prepare them for this kind of work than could yesterday's pioneers.

As a third standard, after goals and preparation, good scholarship uses *appropriate methods*. For the scholarship of teaching and learning, this standard can refer to the kind of learning environment the teacher creates—the teaching practices employed in a course. But it can also refer to the kinds of inquiry the teacher has conducted, which is where disciplinary and subdisciplinary differences in investigative styles surface, and where epistemological issues of practitioner research come most strongly into play. For all comers, however, the quality of the work depends on whether the methods suit the work's context and goals. And the same questions pertain: Have the methods been chosen wisely, applied effectively, and modified judiciously as the project evolves?

And this brings us to the fourth standard of good scholarship: *significant results*. Does the project achieve the goals the scholar lays out? Does it add consequentially to knowledge about teaching and learning in the field? Does it open up additional areas of exploration for the scholar or the scholar's colleagues? The outcome of teaching is student learning, but this outcome is only made evident when the quality of student work is properly evaluated. For scholars of teaching and learning this also requires explanation or interpretation of what accounts for these learning outcomes. What are they a case of? Do the outcomes say something about teaching, learning, or methods of inquiry that was not known before?

And this, of course, leads to the fifth standard in *Scholarship Assessed*: *effective communication*—because for any act of scholarship there are multiple audiences that one can choose to address. The questions to ask about communication are whether the work is presented in a style suitable for its specific audiences. One should also ask if the message is presented with integrity. Clearly *teaching's* primary audiences (if that is the right term) are students, in the classroom, lab, field, and office. But when talking about the *scholarship* of teaching, it is important to underline the necessity of communicating also with peers. Without such communication, a community of discourse about teaching and learning in one's field cannot be established, nor will teaching and learning benefit more generally. This is not an easy task, but, as we have seen in this chapter, much progress has been made.

The final standard is that scholarly work must be accompanied by *reflective critique*. This is the moment when the scholar steps back to think about the results of the project and the response it has provoked, and uses the experience to advance his or her own future work. Has the scholar critically evaluated the project herself? Has she sought comments from colleagues or students? And has she used this evaluation to improve the quality of future work? In the scholarship of teaching and learning, this can involve making specific changes to a course, proposing a shift in the curriculum, revising teaching materials, or designing new investigations that build on or add depth to the old. This process of reflection can also provide the link between projects of different kinds and make them integral parts of some larger intellectual quest.

The standards of *Scholarship Assessed* were offered originally as a language that enables one to see more clearly that discovery, integration, application, and teaching share many qualities as scholarly activities, while leaving sufficient space for variation when applied to different types of projects by people in different fields. For example, the preparation required for the scholarship of teaching and learning is different from that required for discovery in most fields, if only because the actual literatures, resources, and sites for the work are different. Still, it is hard to imagine any scholarly work worthy of the name that did not adhere to these standards. On the most fundamental level, the metric is the same. Clear goals, adequate preparation, appropriate methods, significant results, effective communication, and reflective critique define a core of excellence for all kinds of academic work and thus for the scholarship of teaching and learning.

o

The scholarship of teaching and learning promises to expand college teachers' horizons with a wider range of experience than most faculty members and their immediate colleagues possess. To many educators, however, the word *scholarship* also implies knowledge that builds up as participants make and debate claims about what is the case about this question or that aspect of the world. The kind of knowledge built and exchanged by scholars of teaching and learning is not simply of the anecdotal variety—an interesting, often amusing, and usually unpublished story recounting a classroom problem and what one did to solve it (Salvatori, 2002). To be sure, anecdotes can have an important role in sparking one's pedagogical imagination, communicating the gist of a complicated situation, and suggesting further questions to pursue. But the scholarship of teaching and learning involves making teaching and learning public through systematic documentation, inquiry, and reflection.

The knowledge produced by the scholarship of teaching and learning is, by design, deeply contextual. But as education scholar Virginia Richardson pointed out to us (memorandum to Lee Shulman, January 8, 2004), this same design also allows the larger community to learn more from a project than the initial investigators had learned. Rich representations of practice and robust bodies of evidence allow new questions to be asked of the same data, so that knowledge can continue to build around a particular case. Like scientific and scholarly knowledge more generally, knowledge in teaching and learning may build up incrementally. But it *is* building and practice *is* changing as participation in the scholarship of teaching and learning increases and engagement with the teaching commons grows.

NOTES

1. This epigraph is from Lee Shulman's essay "Taking Learning Seriously" (1999, p. 15). His definition of what constitutes scholarship has been central to CASTL and the larger movement to foster a scholarship of teaching and learning in higher education.
2. Many fields have listservs dedicated to issues in teaching and learning, and listservs dedicated to a wider range of issues in particular scholarly communities often include pedagogical threads. For example, participants on ASAOnet (serving members of the Association for Social Anthropology in Oceania) often solicit colleagues' help in finding appropriate resources and approaches for teaching (http://www.soc.hawaii.edu/asao/pacific/ASAOnet.htm). Web-based resources for teaching are available in most

fields. Historians, for example, can find sample course portfolios on the Web site of the American Historical Association (http://www.historians.org/teaching/AAHE/aahecover.html), microbiologists can find curriculum guidelines, and peer-reviewed resources for undergraduate teaching through the Web site of the American Society for Microbiology (http://www.asm.org/Education/index.asp?bid=1241), engineers can search for innovative educational materials in the digital library, NEEDS—the National Engineering Education Delivery System (http://www.needs.org/needs/; see also Muramatsu and Agogino, 1999), and American studies faculty can consult the American Studies Crossroads project (http://www.georgetown.edu/crossroads/); see also Bass, 1995; Batson and Bass, 1996. Another important project, MERLOT (Multimedia Educational Resource for Learning and Online Teaching) offers materials in multiple subjects as a "free and open resource designed primarily for faculty and students of higher education. Links to online learning materials are collected here along with annotations such as peer reviews and assignments" (http://www.merlot.org/Home.po).

3. Practitioners often help others—faculty, graduate students, even undergraduates—to carry out such work, but they rarely aspire to make the scholarship of teaching and learning a separate subject of instruction.

4. *Wisdom of practice* is a phrase referring to the personal knowledge of practitioners of a skill or profession. Frequently distinguished from, and sometimes denigrated in relation to, an outsider's academic knowledge about the domain in question, the wisdom of practice is nevertheless seen by some scholars as an important "source for understanding the complexities of skilled performance" (Shulman, 2004b [1987], p. 257).

5. For example, when Elaine Showalter, former president of the Modern Language Association, organized a seminar on teaching for graduate students in English at Princeton University, the reading list included book-length guides to teaching, which summarize recent research on learning (Schoenfeld and Magnan's *Mentor in a Manual,* McKeachie's *Teaching Tips,* Lowman's *Mastering the Techniques of Teaching,* and Eble's *The Craft of Teaching*), essays and case studies on classroom discussion (*Teaching and the Case Method,* by Barnes, Christensen, and Hansen and *Education for Judgment,* edited by Christensen, Garvin, and Sweet), one book on research findings (Ramsden's *Learning to Teach in Higher Education*), memoirs of teaching careers (Tompkins's *A Life in School* and Kernan's *In Plato's Cave*), and inspirational works like Palmer's *The Courage to Teach and Brookfield's Becoming a Critically Reflective Teacher* (Showalter, 1999). This comparison of readings about teaching given by Booth and Showalter is drawn from Huber, 2000.

6. In brief, Walvoord (2000) argues, the scholarship of teaching and learning may serve the reader or user as:
    - A heuristic, suggesting approaches the reader may not have considered;
    - A smorgasbord, offering perhaps one or two ideas the reader can use, while ignoring the rest;
    - An example of a basic theory or approach that will work in a new setting if it is adapted or embodied in ways that fit the culture of the new setting;
    - In the aggregate, multiple . . . publications may impart a sense of what is usual, common, or basic to a number of learning situations, but these are likely to come across more like the 'themes' that naturalistic researchers find in disparate data than like 'proofs' of a theory. [p. 2]
7. Participation is voluntary and growing; organizers say that only a small proportion remain reluctant to share content, and for some of these the reason is that the material does not yet feel ready (Margulies, 2004).
8. Bernstein and his colleagues conceived this project as an outgrowth of an earlier project on the peer review of teaching; the latter was launched by the American Association for Higher Education in 1994 as a four-year initiative to engage faculty as professional colleagues in teaching. Twelve universities, including the University of Nebraska-Lincoln, took part, with volunteers from at least three pilot departments on each campus. Bernstein was a participant in the original project, which examined several different ways to foster peer collaboration and review in teaching (Hutchings, 1996), and in a special working group, which focused on the use of course portfolios for this purpose (Hutchings, 1998). On the connection between the AAHE and Nebraska projects, see Huber, 2004.
9. As the KML Web site explains: "If you are interested in documenting teaching as well as students' learning, you have to deal with various kinds of materials and artifacts: a syllabus, course materials, students' work examples, online group discussions, your reflections, etc. However, representing a vast array of materials and artifacts in a succinct and compelling way is a daunting task. The Snapshot Tool, a part of the KEEP Toolkit, helps you efficiently transform your 'stuff' into an appealing and engaging representation." By mid-2004, there were almost fifteen hundred KEEP Toolkit users, including students as well as faculty. For more information, or to use the tool, see http://wwwcarnegiefoundation.org/KML/KEEP/index.htm.

10. Many vocabularies of evaluation are in use for different purposes in higher education. The one proposed in *Scholarship Assessed* was developed in conversation with colleges and universities, granting agencies, university presses, and academic journals, which volunteered materials for the Carnegie Foundation study (see Glassick, Huber, and Maeroff, 1997). Diamond's work with disciplinary associations produced a somewhat different account of what constitutes scholarly work: it requires a high level of discipline-related expertise, breaks new ground or is innovative, can be replicated, can be documented, can be peer reviewed, and has significance or impact (1999). In addition, of course, there is a large literature on quality in teaching itself. One example is Dan Bernstein's elaboration of a collaborative process for the peer review of teaching (2001).

7

AN ACTION AGENDA FOR THE SCHOLARSHIP OF TEACHING AND LEARNING

I had a class where we studied how we learn . . . It flipped a switch, and once it's flipped it can't be turned off.[1]

IT IS A BEAUTIFUL OCTOBER DAY, and Berkeley's Caffe Strada is abuzz with caffeine and conversation. Sitting at the edge of the campus, across the street from a landmark fountain, the coffee shop has become a popular gathering place for chemistry graduate students whose labs are nearby. Indeed, it is the opportunity to meet with two of them that has brought us across the San Francisco Bay for the afternoon. Ian Stewart and Suzanne Blum are, respectively, second- and fourth-year graduate students in chemistry, both of whom studied as undergraduates with Brian Coppola at the University of Michigan—one of the scholars of teaching and learning we have come to know well. Our meeting with them is a chance to learn more about the experience of students in classrooms like Coppola's where learning and teaching are treated as topics of intellectual substance and consequential inquiry.

As our conversation with Blum and Stewart gets under way, it is impossible not to be impressed by the energy and thoughtfulness these young scholars bring to their graduate training. Both balance multiple roles and prodigious amounts of work. Both have roles in two different research labs. Stewart has just completed his orals, and is also student chair of the department's Graduate Student Life Committee. Blum is already looking ahead to postdoctoral and faculty appointments.

Much of what they tell us, given our professed interest in the scholarship of teaching and learning, is about their work in pedagogy. Their experience with this topic goes back to their undergraduate years. As students in Coppola's honors introductory chemistry course at the University of Michigan, they participated in, and then later, as more advanced students, served as tutors for, the structured study groups required for the course (Coppola, Daniels, and Pontrello, 2001).[2] Under Coppola's mentorship, they came to see themselves as teachers, and had a chance to observe other students in the process of learning. Indeed, they told us about what they dubbed "the Brian effect," a view of teaching as "a term-long experiment." "As with molecules," Stewart explains, "there are complex interactions to be understood." One of the lessons they learned from Coppola was about the importance of assessment as a way to understand and then improve the student-learning side of the interaction.

Now, at Berkeley, they find that teaching and assessment are areas where they can make important contributions. Blum has been working as a teaching assistant with a young faculty member who is new to the classroom. Because of her earlier experience with assessment at Michigan, she finds that she can contribute significantly to the design of the course exams and feedback; indeed, her essay about the experience earned her a campuswide teaching award. Not surprisingly, her faculty supervisor is eager to have her input, in part because it is so helpful but also because he knows Coppola's reputation as a scholar of teaching and learning.

Stewart, too, finds the experience he gained at Michigan in demand at Berkeley. Like most first-year graduate students in the program, he started as a teaching assistant for an introductory undergraduate course. Now, in his second year (and "following in Suzanne's footsteps"), his role is more involved, teaching an advanced undergraduate course with an assistant professor who is also his adviser. This means significant responsibility for the creation of problem sets and exams, and for the development of a literature-based semester project.

Blum's and Stewart's experience with Coppola and with subsequent pedagogical work not only gives them a leg up as future professors but also makes them better chemists. "Teaching and chemistry make use of the same set of tools," Stewart tells us, an insight he confesses would not have been so clear if he had not done both as an undergraduate. He believes that his participation in Coppola's pedagogical and curricular work helped deepen his understanding of chemistry—and "not just because of time on task" (the time spent teaching chemistry to others) but because he came to see the similarities between the two, "so that doing one helped you understand the other; both involve a form of problem solving" (see Huber, 2004).

The story we heard from Stewart and Blum at Caffe Strada is partly a story about learning to teach. The two would make admirable "poster people" for programs that prepare students for careers as faculty. And they remind us that useful preparation can begin even before graduate school. But, just as important, it is a story about learning to learn. Indeed, what is most striking to us is the capacity of these young chemists to talk about their own experience as learners, to reflect on their educational experiences, to "go meta" as learners in the same way that the scholarship of teaching and learning asks teachers to do with teaching (Hutchings and Shulman, 1999). In this way, their experience holds a powerful lesson: classrooms like Coppola's where teachers are actively investigating what transpires in their interactions with students, and sharing what they learn with others who can build on it, are likely to be classrooms where students, too, get smarter about learning. Moving in ever-wider circles, the scholarship of teaching and learning invites not only teachers but also students into a larger commons that can support powerful learning through a lifetime.

Learning About Learning

The need for students to understand their own learning—to "go meta"—is increasingly on higher education's radar screen—for instance, in the call for "intentional learning" in *Greater Expectations,* the 2002 report from the Association of American Colleges and Universities. It is a view of learning with a long history, part of the tradition of liberal education, which has always valued (though perhaps not always actively and explicitly taught for) the ability to make sense of one's own learning, and to take charge of it in ways that lead to integration and coherence.[3] Intentional learners approach learning with high levels of self-awareness, understanding their own processes and goals as learners, and making choices (one hopes) that promote connections and depth of understanding. They know how to monitor and focus their efforts—how to make the most of their study time, to practice new skills, to ask probing questions. They are, if you will, on the road to a lifetime of learning in just the way that Blum and Stewart obviously are.

This vision of education reflects many lines of research and practice. In adult and professional education, for example, one finds several decades of attention to *self-directed learning* (Brookfield, 1986; Sabral, 1997; Taylor and Burgess, 1995). Advocates of this approach point to the power of explicit goals in which students are personally invested. A related line of work goes by the label of *learning how to learn.* A recent volume on new classroom approaches describes three abilities associated with this phrase: how to be a better student, how to conduct inquiry and construct knowledge in particular disciplines or fields, and how to be a self-directing learner (Fink, 2003).

Work from cognitive science, which is increasingly invoked in discussions of teaching and learning (Bransford, Brown, and Cocking, 1999; Halpern and Hakel, 2003) is relevant as well. Most notable is the emphasis on metacognition, which entails knowing what one knows and does not know, predicting outcomes, planning ahead, efficiently apportioning time and cognitive resources, and monitoring one's efforts to solve a problem or to learn (Glaser, 1984).

The capacities for learning that we saw in Blum's and Stewart's trajectory as students also bring to mind the extensive work on reflection that dates (at least) from Dewey. Donald Schön's work on reflective practice, for instance, highlights the connection between thought and action as a key foundation for learning in which "doing and thinking are complementary" (1983, p. 280). Through reflection, Schön argues, we "surface and criticize the tacit understandings that have grown up around the repetitive experiences of a specialized practice, and can make new sense of . . . situations of uncertainty or uniqueness" (1983, p. 61). Schön's work focuses primarily on professional education and practice, but the role of reflection in undergraduate education has also garnered attention. For instance, a current project of the Carnegie Foundation has identified structured reflection as one of six pedagogies useful in preparing students for political engagement.[4] In composition studies, reflection is seen as a key component in the writing process and a necessary ingredient, therefore, in the teaching of writing (Yancey, 1998; Cambridge and Williams, 1998).

Reflection. Metacognition. Learning how to learn. Whatever the language or lineage, the idea of making students more intentional, self-aware, and purposeful about their studies is a powerful one. Such processes are key to deeper, more integrative learning, and to motivation. As illustrated by the stories told by Blum and Stewart, they are also goals that are particularly well-served when faculty take up the scholarship of teaching and learning.

Inviting Students into the Teaching Commons

We have been especially struck by the interest among those who have taken up the scholarship of teaching and learning in developing ways to help students demystify the process of academic learning. Indeed, an important lesson from the movement thus far is that when faculty begin to investigate and document their work as teachers (and especially their impact on students' learning) they also find themselves wanting to share their insights with students—to let students in on why they do what they do, and, as some of our colleagues have taken to saying, to stop "hiding the ball." This shift is evident, for instance, at Western Washington University, where, as part of its campus initiative on the scholarship of teaching and learning, the institution created a course in which students explore their own processes as learners. The course has now gone through several iterations: the current version is entitled Civil Discourse as Engaged Learning, which includes a practicum in the institution's Teaching-Learning Academy with faculty and staff. The power of the experience is evident in the epigraph from the Western Washington student that begins this chapter: "I had a class where we studied how we learn. . . . It flipped a switch, and once it's flipped it can't be turned off" (Skogsberg, 2004). Not surprisingly, the course has been much in demand by students, and we have been impressed by its impact, in turn, on the larger campus culture (Werder, 2004).

Students in a microbiology course taught by Heidi Elmendorf, a scholar of teaching and learning at Georgetown University, have had a different but also very powerful experience. One of the questions Elmendorf is investigating is what happens to undergraduates' science learning when they have a chance to teach the material they themselves are newly encountering. In a course for non-majors entitled Shall the Microbes Inherit the Earth? Elmendorf offers students the option of teaching science to elementary school children in the Washington, D.C., public schools, instead of participating in the typical laboratory experience; this means designing the lessons as well as conducting them, and it is, in fact, the structuring of knowledge *in order to teach it* that Elmendorf sees as especially powerful for these undergraduates. Though her research is still in progress and she is careful not to make grand claims about which approach works best, her interviews with students who have chosen the teaching option are striking in what they say about learning. One student, for example, talks about how the teaching experience has made him "a traveler to a foreign land," where "you notice things" about science that scientists themselves do not (Elmendorf, 2004). In short, the teaching that Elmendorf's students do in elementary school classrooms helps them to "go meta" on their own learning back on campus.[5]

A different approach to helping students become savvier, more self-aware learners and thinkers appears in the work of a faculty member in English. For Cynthia Scheinberg at Mills College, the key is making one's goals as an educator more visible and explicit for students (see Collins, Brown, and Holum, 1991). Scheinberg argues that class discussion is an activity in which the intellectual habits necessary for good writing (developing ideas, making transitions, clarifying terms, and so forth) are powerfully embodied. As teachers, she says, "Many of us become adept at directing conversation, using the role of discussion leader to synthesize reading assignments, pose probing questions that spark critical thinking, create transitions between different ideas, offer links and related references for new direction. Often, we enter the class with a larger theme for structuring discussion, and produce conversation summaries at the end of class. In short, we become managers of content and ideas, shapers of the larger discourse; it is a role many of us (myself included) enjoy immensely" (Scheinberg, 2003, p. 2). The problem, as Scheinberg sees it, is that when faculty become "too good at facilitation" students are robbed of the chance to develop these skills for themselves.

With this diagnosis in mind, Scheinberg sets out to draw attention to such skills through what she calls Conversacolor, an activity that helps students become aware of the various moves required in intellectual exchange—be it introducing a new idea, building on someone else's point, raising a question, or even changing the topic. Like Elmendorf's experiments with teaching as a form of learning, Scheinberg's approach aims to make students smarter about their own learning, and to let them in on the tricks of the academic trade rather than "perpetuate the misconception that the life of the mind is a secret society for which only an elite few qualify" (Graff, 2003, p. 1). Instead of treating students as objects of investigation, scholars of teaching and learning like Scheinberg and Elmendorf involve students in activities that invite questions about learning and that provide a more sophisticated map of the intellectual arts. In so doing, they invite students into the teaching commons.

The Need for Pedagogical Intelligence

The desire to bring students into the commons by making them more self-aware, intentional learners is not new, but the need to do so is, we would argue, more pressing than ever.[6] For one thing, students' educational experiences are increasingly likely to be "uncommon," in the sense that they are often fragmented and disconnected. More and more students are now attending several institutions over their college career. The exact numbers of students who do so nationwide is not known, but one study indicates that fully half of the bachelor's degree recipients in 1992–93 took courses at more than one college or university (sometimes concurrently), and 20 percent attended at least three (McCormick, 2003, p. 17). Some students transfer from two- to four-year institutions, others experiment with their first college to see if they like it and then transfer to another, some accelerate their programs by taking one or two terms elsewhere, others just take a supplementary course or two. Some educators see this trend as a reflection of more consumerist attitudes on the part of today's students (Levine and Cureton, 1998; Fallon, 2002). Whatever the causes, these "swirling" patterns of enrollment make it increasingly important for students to take control of their own learning. Accordingly, many institutions are creating more integrated, linked experiences for their undergraduates, but approaches that develop students' capacity to make connections for *themselves* are also needed (see Huber and Hutchings, 2005; Association of American Colleges and Universities, 2002; Schneider and Schoenberg, 1999).

The need for this capacity is not simply a function of changed enrollment patterns. It reflects the shifting conditions of knowledge itself. The academic disciplines today are less bounded, with new areas of scientific knowledge emerging on the borders of old ones, and the humanities and social sciences engaged in lively trade of concepts, methods, and even subject matter (Geertz, 1983; Bender and Schorske, 1997; Gallison, 1997). Technology and globalization are transforming knowledge practices in all the disciplines, professions, and arts (Gibbons and Associates, 1994). Indeed, we are awash in information in all areas of life.

The workplace, too, has been transformed. Today's knowledge society places a premium on higher education, making college a virtual necessity for students aspiring to a middle-class style of life. With flexibility and mobility the keywords of the new economy, people can no longer count on a long career with the same employer or even in the same line of work. Students are now advised that the knowledge they gain in their majors will not be useful for long unless coupled with skills and dispositions that enhance their ability to find and take advantage of new opportunities when the need arises. *Lifelong learning* may be a buzzword, but it is also increasingly a necessity—and not a simple one.

If students today would benefit from taking a more intentional, deliberative, and reflective stance toward learning, the same is true for all of us. Scientific and technological development and globalization have made everything more complex, bringing many advantages to the fortunate but also exacerbating inequalities and elevating risk for all. This is no longer a world where it is easy to feel in control or able to affect what is happening in one's neighborhood, much less in the nation or the world. But by the same token one's own actions—even the choice of food, clothing, and car—have immediate consequences for those far away (Giddens, 1994).

These conditions require sophisticated moral judgment and practical reasoning (Sullivan, 2002). To participate responsibly, citizens today must be able to synthesize learning from a wide array of sources, learn from experience, and make productive connections between theory and practice.

As we move into the twenty-first century, all of us need to be smarter learners. We need ways of thinking about ourselves as learners, and about how we learn, to get us through the fast-moving, complex swirl of ingredients that is contemporary life. There is much talk today about knowledge workers (see Austin, 2002; McSherry, 2001), but we would argue that knowledge workers need also to be *pedagogical thinkers,* able to construct for themselves (and sometimes for others) activities that allow learning, growth, and change. The notion of multiple intelligences has had wide play for the last several decades. Howard Gardner (1983) postulates a whole set of them: linguistic, musical, logical-mathematical, spatial, body-kinesthetic, and personal intelligences. Daniel Goleman popularized the idea of an emotional intelligence (1995). Some might argue that the word *intelligence* invites misunderstanding, because it seems to suggest traits that are inherited and static. But the idea that multiple capacities and dispositions are possible, and, indeed, needed to function effectively in the world is a right one, and we would propose that yet another is needed as well, a *pedagogical intelligence,* which is not only for teachers, or even for students in the narrow sense, but for everyone (Hutchings, 2005).

Recommendations

What will it take to foster this kind of intelligence about teaching and learning? What established strategies and next steps will help build a commons to support such a vision—one that will be valued and used to improve what goes on in classrooms and other settings where learning occurs?

The scholarship of teaching and learning has achieved considerable momentum, but continued leadership and commitment will clearly be needed in many quarters—in the classroom and at the department and program level; from campus administrative leadership, but also from disciplinary and professional societies; from funders and from governing and accrediting boards; and, indeed, from all who care about our society's capacity for learning over time.

As we look ahead, we see five areas of action that promise to yield significant benefits:

A first need is to **establish more and better occasions to talk about learning.** This sounds simple but it isn't. Campus conversations about learning often take place on the edges of campus life, and in ad hoc ways that cannot be sustained or built on. Structures and occasions are needed to bring people together on campus for sustained, substantive, constructive discussion about learning and how to improve it. Here are some possibilities for doing this:

- Individual faculty experimenting with particular pedagogies can establish working groups in which they share questions, practices, data, tools, and opportunities for connecting with colleagues beyond the campus. Such efforts are more likely to succeed when given institutional support in the form of modest funding, library resources, help with technology—and food.
- At the department level, time can be set aside on a regular basis for discussion of student learning in the program. Models for such work can be found in the University of Michigan mathematics department with its seminar on student understanding, or the Gustavus Adolphus history department with its work focused on a text about the learning and understanding of history as a discipline. Inviting colleagues from related disciplines (on the home campus or nearby) can enrich the conversation. Documenting what happens and what is learned lends intellectual gravitas to the process and makes its fruits more broadly useful.
- Campuses might establish a seminar that brings together faculty and others who share responsibility for the educational experience, to identify questions about their students' learning, design studies to explore those questions, share their findings in regular meetings over the course of a year or more, and catalyze action that builds on findings. Harvard University's Assessment Seminars provide a model for such an approach, and one whose impact was greatly expanded by the production of highly readable, broadly circulated publications on results and outcomes.

Second, **students need to be part of the discussion about learning.** At its best, academic advising provides a forum for students to talk about their educational experience, but advising is not enough. Students need *multiple* venues to think and talk together—and to others inside and outside of the academy—about their learning. Some of this should occur in classes (nothing sends a stronger signal about what matters). For undergraduates, likely candidates include first-year seminars and capstone courses, which offer occasions to help students "go meta" with their learning; for graduate students, seminars on the pedagogy of the field offer a chance to talk about learning. But students gain—and add—powerful new insights when they participate in broader campus and departmental forums on learning as well—the kinds of occasions highlighted in our first recommendation. Possibilities for involving students in serious talk about learning include the following:

- Students can work with faculty to investigate questions about learning and teaching. This kind of collaboration might take the form of an undergraduate research experience organized around a scholarship of teaching and learning project; a number of CASTL Scholars involved their students as coinvestigators. Student involvement is also a hallmark of the Harvard Assessment Seminars, where both undergraduate and graduate students conducted focus groups, administered surveys, and contributed to the analysis of data. The experience gave them new lenses for looking at their own education, and along the way helped hone their research skills.
- Campuses might create a course or courses in which students have a chance to study their own learning and how to improve it. Student interest in such opportunities, though hardly standard fare, turns out to be high in some settings. Western Washington University found students eager to enroll in the seminar they created as part of their involvement in CASTL; the course aims to make students more self-aware, active participants in their own learning, and more reflective about what it takes to create a culture of learning in the institution. Courses like this can be even more powerful when their goals and themes are reinforced and infused in the wider curriculum, from the first-year experience, through milestones in the middle years, to the senior capstone or culminating project.
- Students can learn about learning by serving as mentors, tutors, and teachers of other students. Such arrangements are increasingly in evidence—for instance, in honors chemistry at the University of Michigan where students who have already taken the course return as tutors to those currently enrolled. A different model but with similar impact is the experience of Heidi Elmendorf's Georgetown University students teaching biology to school children in Washington, D.C.

A third need is to **recognize teaching as substantive, intellectual work.** Taking *learning* seriously, in the ways suggested by our first two recommendations, means taking *teaching* seriously as well. Too often teaching is treated as a matter of technique, as if technique alone can bring improvement. On the contrary. Teaching will be advanced when it is seen as intellectual work inviting careful deliberation among those who constitute the professional community and who take responsibility, as professionals in all fields must do, for improving the quality of the enterprise. For example:

- Individual faculty need resources of time and money to do their work as scholars of teaching and learning. With expectations of faculty already multiplying on many campuses, the scholarship of teaching and learning cannot simply be added to the list, and certainly it should not be required. The mechanisms of support available for more traditional forms of research—small grants, sabbaticals, assistance with grant writing, travel money—are also necessary ingredients in serious work on teaching and learning. Sometimes such work requires a reduction in teaching itself, which should be seen as an institutional investment in improvement. Many CASTL Scholars received a reduced teaching load in order to do a project that subsequently benefited their own students, colleagues, and campuses, as well as contributing to the wider teaching commons. Especially important are forms of support that connect faculty to others, on their campus and beyond, who are engaging in similar work.
- Campuses would do well to examine their infrastructure for professional development, and especially how it supports teaching. A new faculty orientation may include a strong focus on instruction, for instance, but opportunities for faculty to do serious intellectual work as teachers must run throughout the career, from hiring to posttenure review. Many campus offices can contribute. The office of assessment may be important; the office of institutional research was a key partner in Dennis Jacobs' study of introductory chemistry at Notre Dame. On many campuses a center for teaching provides the backbone for ongoing efforts toward faculty's development as scholars of teaching and learning. Such centers should be centrally located and well-funded to signal the importance of teaching in the intellectual climate of the campus.
- Scholars of teaching and learning need to receive intellectual credit for their efforts. This need is met in the discipline-based research arena by elaborate conventions for citation, quotation, and acknowledgment. Such conventions must be developed around the scholarship of teaching and learning as well.

- Institutional rewards must be forthcoming, too. This means bringing policies and practices for promotion and tenure into alignment with new ideas about the scholarly work of teaching, as many institutions have begun to do. But promotion and tenure are only part of the picture. The value of the scholarship of teaching and learning to the institution may be signaled in various ways at various points in the career: hiring, probationary review, posttenure review, and teaching awards, to name just a few of the possibilities. All of these evaluations can be strengthened by appropriate strategies for peer review.
- The scholarship of teaching and learning should be an important component of graduate education. Exposure to existing pedagogical scholarship as well as involvement in the process of classroom inquiry sends a powerful signal to graduate students that teaching is significant intellectual work and a valued part of professional life. Departments on a growing number of research universities are making a place for such work, sometimes (as in the chemistry department at the University of Michigan) through partnerships with the college of education.

Fourth, we must push forward with **new genres and forms to document the work of teaching and learning.** For teaching to advance as a field that strengthens student learning, classroom practices must be captured in ways that can be widely shared, critiqued, and built on. Toward this end, higher education must continue to develop and refine new ways of going public with the work of teaching and learning. Traditional forms of publication—journal articles, books, and so forth—have an important role to play, but the commons must also include forms and formats that capture more of teaching's contexts and complexity. Steps toward meeting this need include the following:

- Faculty who are exploring their teaching and their students' learning may wish to experiment with new tools for documenting that work through multimedia. Electronic course portfolios are one possibility. The MIT OpenCourseWare project offers another model. Yet a third, aimed at producing more distilled, simpler representations, is the "snapshot tool" available as part of the KEEP Toolkit (KEEP stands for Knowledge Exchange, Exhibition, and Presentation) developed by the Carnegie Foundation's Knowledge Media Laboratory. Built around a flexible template for representing the questions, evidence, outcomes, and implications of work in the scholarship of teaching and learning, the snapshot tool is free and available to all.

- Campuses should bring their resources for instructional technology to bear on the scholarship of teaching and learning. There is much to be gained by working with faculty to document new approaches in the classroom in ways that colleagues can access and understand through video, electronic course materials, samples of student work, and other artifacts and reflective commentaries that can be captured using new media. Georgetown University's Center for New Designs in Learning and Scholarship, which houses the Visible Knowledge Project (http://crossroads.georgetown.edu/vkp/), has embraced this agenda in a bold way that may be a suggestive model for other campuses.
- Foundations should support projects in the scholarship of teaching and learning and also *require* that the work they fund be documented and preserved in ways that can be used by others. For example, The William and Flora Hewlett Foundation is rethinking grant giving with a sharper eye to knowledge building, and is looking for ways to use new media to capture project outcomes in ways that can be easily shared. Similarly, many of the campuses involved in Carnegie Foundation programs are developing multimedia snapshots to document their work, and in some cases to report to funders about what they have done.

Fifth, higher education should help **build and maintain the infrastructure needed to make pedagogical work of high quality available and accessible to all.** Efforts by individuals to support and further the scholarship of teaching and learning can only go so far. Thus, we wish to point as well toward the need for structures and initiatives that will connect those seeking to move ahead with this work. Building the teaching commons will require additional mechanisms for connection, coordination, and stewardship.

- There is a need for the development and funding of efforts that bring people from different campuses and disciplines together to work on important questions about teaching and student learning. We have named some that have contributed to the growth of such communities in recent years: the multicampus project on course portfolios based at the University of Nebraska, for instance; the Visible Knowledge Project headquartered at Georgetown University; efforts undertaken by scholarly and professional societies; and of course the work of The Carnegie Foundation for the Advancement of Teaching. Many others, including initiatives like the Center for the Integration of Research, Teaching, and Learning and the Center for the Advancement of Engineering Education funded by the National Science Foundation, are creating opportunities for new participants to join in the work. More are needed.

- New venues and outlets for sharing the scholarship of teaching and learning must be created. Several scholarly societies have established new journals for this purpose, others have created teaching-focused conferences. Some are using their Web sites to host listserv discussions about teaching and learning or to post (and peer-review) electronic portfolios focused on the teaching of the field. Because the disciplines and professional fields are the source of such powerful signals about what counts—what is scholarly—their efforts to make high-quality pedagogical scholarship available to the community hold special promise.
- Repositories and maps must be created through which the work of scholars of teaching and learning can be located and used. Campus libraries might become repositories for local work on teaching—perhaps documented in multimedia formats and available online. Faculty could then learn about the work of a colleague down the hall by searching the collection. And because almost all academic libraries today are part of larger, multicampus databases, local collections of pedagogical work might then be linked and made accessible in a larger network. Tools and technologies that can be used to generate and share data about student learning across sites will be especially important in advancing this vision.
- Higher education should mount a fierce resistance to the commercialization and privatization of pedagogical work. As noted in Chapter One, there is a long history of enclosure blocking the commons off from ready access; work that was once available to all is literally or metaphorically fenced, policed, privatized, or priced in ways that do not serve the larger, public good. This trend is already well on its way in the academy, with understandings about who owns what (for instance, course materials) increasingly a matter of hot debate. Those of us committed to the teaching mission of higher education must resist this trend, seeking ways to make new pedagogical practices, tools, and understandings broadly available—not only *building* the teaching commons but protecting it and ensuring access.

Big Ideas for the Future

As we write this final chapter, a year has passed since we visited with Suzanne Blum and Ian Stewart at Caffe Strada. Blum has now completed her doctoral work and gone on to a postdoc at Harvard. Stewart is moving along toward his degree and thinking more intently about career possibilities (perhaps in academe, perhaps not) in which he can further his scientific and pedagogical interests (Ian Stewart, e-mail to the authors, October 28, 2004). We are grateful to both of them for giving us a glimpse into their busy and productive lives, and, having had that glimpse, it is hard, of course, to resist imagining where they will be and what they will be doing in five, ten, even twenty years. As accomplished researchers in their respective subfields in chemistry who are also deeply engaged by questions about student learning and committed to the scholarship of teaching and learning, will they find an academic home and culture in which these two strands of interest can be pursued, maybe even braided together, and valued? Will the academy have the good sense to make such places? One of our goals as we began writing this book was to look back at the evolution of the scholarship of teaching and learning in order to look ahead and strategize about its possibilities. So, what *are* those possibilities? What will be the character and place of the scholarship of teaching and learning in five, ten, even twenty years? Table 7.1 takes a look at how CASTL Scholars see the future.

One possibility is that the scholarship of teaching and learning will simply disappear and leave no trace. Perhaps predictably, only 2 percent of CASTL Scholars believe this will happen; as individuals who have invested time and effort in such work, they are, in a way, *themselves,* the "trace" and they have no plans to disappear. Many of them are eloquent in describing the difference that the scholarship of teaching and learning has made in their lives, in their sense of themselves, and in their interactions with students and colleagues. Some have moved on to administrative positions in order to provide more vigorous leadership and support for the scholarship of teaching and learning; some have been hired away from their former institutions by places that are seeking out such scholars and enticing them with attractive arrangements and opportunities.

At this point, such developments are, admittedly, the exception rather than the rule, but 45 percent of CASTL Scholars believe that the scholarship of teaching and learning will become "a fully legitimate, 'counted' kind of scholarly work" on their campus in five to ten years; 32 percent say this will happen in ten to twenty years. Most notably, perhaps, half say that the scholarship of teaching and learning will, in five to ten years,

Table 7.1. Predictions for the Future of the Scholarship of Teaching and Learning

	Percent of Respondents			
	5–10 Years	10–20 Years	20+ Years	Never
It will become a fully legitimate, "counted" kind of scholarly work on my campus.	45	32	5	11
It will become a respected specialty in my discipline or professional field.	56	26	4	9
It will become an expectation of all faculty at various points in their careers, institutionalized through campus policies.	17	26	20	44
It will contribute to widespread changes in how students learn in postsecondary classrooms.	50	32	12	2
It will disappear and leave no trace.	2	0	0	91
It will become a form of accountability used against faculty.	17	9	3	56

Source: *Cox, Huber, and Hutchings, CASTL Scholars Survey 2004.*

"contribute to widespread changes in how students learn in postsecondary classrooms" (Cox, Huber, and Hutchings, 2004). Of course that means that another half do *not* hold out such hope, at least not in that time frame. And we suspect that those outside the CASTL circle are likely to be less sanguine about the movement's sticking power and impact. Still, it is notable that a significant number of academic administrators report growth in the movement: 62 percent of provosts responding to a 2002 survey by the American Association for Higher Education report that faculty involvement in the scholarship of teaching is on the rise (O'Meara, 2005, p. 269).

As always, the numbers tell a mixed story—or, rather, several stories—and there are reasons to be hopeful and to be skeptical.[7] What most strikes us, stepping back from the details, is that in asking about the future, one must return to the question of definitions because the future of this movement depends on how it is described, and especially how it is framed and represented to those (and there are many) who are not sure what it points to, or what it implies for them and their communities. Who feels welcomed, and who excluded?

Early on in the CASTL program, we asked campuses to begin their work by crafting a definition of the scholarship of teaching and learning that would make sense in their particular culture.[8] More recently, we asked CASTL Scholars to tell us how they talk about their work when addressing new audiences. Predictably, some have found this a challenge. "I have tried to avoid mentioning that I do it—to all but a select few friends," one confesses. It is, opines another, "very difficult to explain." But many have found useful and appealing formulations. "I put the emphasis on the process of being as discerning about what is learned as we are about what is taught," says Anita Salem, a mathematician in the group (Response to CASTL Scholars Survey, 2004). In a similar spirit, Mariolina Salvatori (whose work is featured in Chapter Three) proposes that the "most salient characteristic of the scholarship of teaching . . . is unprecedented attentiveness to students' work, their cultural capital, and their learning as a litmus test for the theories that inform a teacher's approach." She goes on: "This focus has fostered an understanding of the classroom as a site where student voices are actually heard, where their knowledges are actually acknowledged and engaged, where teachers reconceive teaching and themselves as they learn to ask and to address simple but consequential questions like, what does it mean for me to teach *this* text with *this* approach to *this* population of students at *this* time in *this* classroom?" (Salvatori, 2002, p. 298).

Statements like these (there are many more we could quote) are especially appealing, in our view, because they allow for a broad range of practices, value both the doing of the work and the products and results it leads to, and make a space for efforts that can be either highly elaborated or more modest, qualitative or quantitative (often both), focused on a large sample perhaps tracked over time or on a single assignment or the work of just one student, documented on a Web site, shared in a workshop, or reported in an article or book. All of these, in our big-tent view of the scholarship of teaching and learning, belong in the commons, where they can, as it were, rub up against an even broader range of work, work that is *not* the scholarship of teaching and learning (ours is a big tent, but it is not the whole universe) but that extends and deepens its possibilities. Thus, on one end of what might be seen as a continuum, one finds "just plain" good teaching, or "scholarly teaching" as some have called it (Hutchings and Shulman, 1999), and on the other end, more basic research of the kind reported, for instance, in *How People Learn* (Bransford, Brown, and Cocking, 1999). The point and the power of the commons, then, is to do what its name implies: constitute a shared space, a lingua franca, a network of intersections and connections across otherwise diverse practices and communities.

What we are saying here is that the promise of the scholarship of teaching and learning will best be met by focusing on the big ideas that run through and animate the broader commons: that teaching is intellectual work, that learning poses tough problems that require careful investigation and "unprecedented attentiveness," as Salvatori puts it, that rich evidence about learning needs to guide thoughtful improvement, that the important work of education should not disappear like dry ice but, as Shulman argues, be made visible and sharable and useful for others, including those *beyond* the academy, who are committed to powerful learning.

Big ideas need time and space to play themselves out. They are easy to say but often hard to understand at a deep level, and hard to enact. But we believe these ideas are taking hold today, in the academy and beyond, as learning is increasingly recognized to be a lifetime project. Many wonderful, committed people have been attracted to this work; they have found colleagues and audiences in places they might not otherwise have looked or known about. Through the scholarship of teaching and learning, they have also pursued significant improvements in their own and others' classrooms. Such work has pushed inquiry in new and promising directions. We hope readers of this volume will be moved to join the journey, to engage with and contribute to the rich and growing teaching commons.

NOTES

1. This epigraph comes from a presentation by Erik Skogsberg, a student at Western Washington University, to the AAHE Summer Academy in Stowe, Vermont, July 2004. He is speaking about his experience in a course designed by his campus to involve students in the scholarship of teaching and learning. For more information, see Werder, Redmond, Purdue, and Patrick (2003). Also see Werder's chapter in the 2004 volume from AAHE, *Campus Progress*.
2. In 1994, the University of Michigan chemistry department introduced an honors elective linked to both terms of its thousand-student first-year organic chemistry course. Students selecting this option participate in all regular course elements (lecture, lab, and recitation) but also meet two evening hours a week for collaborative learning sessions led by junior and

senior undergraduate student leaders. These structured study groups are shaped by the concept of reciprocal teaching and allow students to try out ideas, to teach one another, and to reflect on and explain their own learning. Group leaders, who previously took the course themselves, practice similar skills at a higher level. One leader reflects on the experience as follows: "The most important lesson I learned was that the 'teacher' is never just an instructor but a student as well for the rest of their life" (Coppola, Daniels, and Pontrello, 2001, p. 119).

3. We have drawn much of this section from our monograph, *Integrative Learning: Mapping the Terrain* (Huber and Hutchings, 2004).

4. The Political Engagement Project is a three-year collaborative study of twenty-one diverse courses and programs that focus on political engagement. The study is documenting the goals and pedagogies of the participating courses and programs, students' perspectives on their experiences in the programs, and the impact of these experiences on key dimensions of political engagement such as knowledge and understanding, sense of efficacy, and political identity. In addition to this overarching study, a number of participating faculty and program leaders are conducting investigations into distinctive features of their courses and programs. (See the Web site at http://www.carnegiefoundation.org/PEP/index.htm.)

5. Elmendorf is also working with several colleagues on a capstone experience for biology majors (a series of three courses) in which teaching in the Washington, D.C., public schools is offered as an option. The option appeals, as one student explains, because it will "force me to be creative and actually require me to know what I have learned" (Bass, R., 2004).

6. We draw here, as well, on our integrative learning monograph (Huber and Hutchings, 2005).

7. One of the issues that arises in our survey of CASTL Scholars is the relationship between the scholarship of teaching and learning and the accountability movement. Several respondents worry that, in the words of one, "the scholarship of teaching and learning could be hijacked . . . to make higher education accountable." But where some see trouble, one, at least, sees possibility. Refusing to assume that "accountability is hostile to faculty," this respondent notes, "It could be a form of accountability *for* faculty." Certainly this perspective is congruent with Carnegie's notion of an ethic of inquiry. Shulman has argued that the scholarship of teaching and learning is a way of enacting faculty's responsibility as professional educators. It is accountability from the inside, bottom up, rather than a mandate from the outside (Hutchings, 2000; Shulman, 2000a).

8. The CASTL Campus Program, asked institutions to begin their process by having a "campus conversation" about a "sacrificial definition" of the scholarship of teaching and learning: "The scholarship of teaching is problem posing about an issue of teaching or learning, study of the problem through methods appropriate to disciplinary epistemologies, applications of results to practice, communication of results, self-reflection, and peer review." The resulting definitions often reflect campus mission and culture, for instance with research universities more inclined to focus on formal research, publication, and the like. For campus reports on this work, see *Campus Progress: Supporting the Scholarship of Teaching and Learning* (Cambridge, 2004).

Exhibit 7.1 Action Agenda for the Scholarship of Teaching and Learning

- A first area for action is to **establish more and better occasions to talk about learning.** What's needed are structures and occasions that bring people on campus together for sustained, substantive, constructive discussion about learning and how to improve it. These can include working groups for individual faculty experimenting with particular pedagogies; departmental discussions of student learning in their programs; or seminars for those who share responsibility for the educational experience to identify questions about their students' learning, design studies to explore those questions, share their findings in regular meetings over the course of a year or more, and catalyze action that builds on findings.

- Second, **students need to be part of the discussion about learning.** At its best, academic advising provides a forum for students to talk about their educational experience, but advising is not enough. Students need *multiple* venues to think and talk together—and to others inside and outside of the academy—about their learning. Some of this should occur in classes (nothing sends a stronger signal about what matters). But students can also learn about learning by serving as mentors, tutors, and teachers of other students, as collaborators with faculty investigating questions about learning and teaching, and as participants in broader campus and departmental forums on learning, as well.

- A third need is to **recognize teaching as substantive, intellectual work.** Taking *learning* seriously means taking *teaching* seriously, as well. Teaching will be advanced when it is seen as intellectual work inviting careful deliberation among those who constitute the professional community and who take responsibility, as professionals in all fields must do, for improving the quality of the enterprise. Scholars of teaching and learning need resources of time and money to do their work, a strong campus infrastructure to support teaching, intellectual credit and institutional reward for their efforts, and better preparation for pedagogical scholarship as a component of graduate training.

- Fourth, we must push forward with **new genres and forms to document the work of teaching and learning.** For teaching to advance as a field in ways that strengthen student learning, classroom practices must be captured in ways that can be widely shared, critiqued, and built upon. Toward this end, higher education must continue to develop and refine new ways of going public with the work of teaching and learning. Traditional forms of publication—journal articles, books, and so forth—have an important role to play, but the commons must also include forms and formats that capture more of teaching's contexts and complexity.

- Fifth, higher education should help **build and maintain the infrastructure needed to make pedagogical work of high quality available and accessible to all.** There is a need for the development and funding of efforts that bring people together from different institutions, disciplines, and countries, for exchange around important questions about teaching and student learning, for new venues and outlets for sharing the scholarship of teaching and learning, for the creation and maintenance of repositories and maps through which this work can be located and used, and for fierce resistance to the commercialization and privatization of pedagogical work. All who are committed to the teaching mission of higher education must seek ways to make new pedagogical practices, tools, and understandings broadly available, thus building the pedagogical commons, protecting it, and ensuring access.

APPENDIX: SURVEY OF CASTL SCHOLARS

Rebecca Cox, Mary Taylor Huber, and Pat Hutchings

2004 Survey of CASTL Scholars

National Fellowship Winners, 1998–2004

The Carnegie Academy for the Scholarship of Teaching and Learning

THIS SURVEY OF five cohorts of CASTL Scholars was designed to explore various aspects of their experience as scholars of teaching and learning: their motivations, dilemmas, and satisfactions as individuals undertaking this work; their departmental, institutional, and disciplinary contexts and how those contexts may be changing; and the impact of their work on others, including students. Our goal was to paint a broad-brush picture of the scholarship of teaching and learning as it has played itself out, over a number of years, in the lives of professionals who embrace it.

The questionnaire was initially drafted during summer 2003, went through a series of revisions during the fall based on feedback from Carnegie Foundation staff experienced with survey research, and from a pilot distribution to a few CASTL scholars. The final version was then sent by e-mail during the second week of January 2004 to every participant (to that date) in CASTL's higher education program ($n = 137$). With a few gentle reminders, most returned their questionnaires by mid-February 2004.

A total of 114 CASTL Scholars responded to the survey, for a response rate of 83 percent. The majority of respondents (52 percent) were employed at doctoral-level institutions during the 2003–04 academic year, 23 percent were at master's colleges and universities, 14 percent at baccalaureate colleges, and 8 percent at community colleges. (The other

3 percent were from specialized or overseas institutions.) Most respondents described themselves as tenured professors (80 percent), with a rank of either associate professor (32 percent) or full professor (48 percent).

Representing a range of disciplinary backgrounds, respondents were evenly distributed among departments in arts and humanities; social sciences; math, science, and engineering; education and other professional fields.

In reading the results on the survey form, please note that percentages for each question total 100 percent only when all respondents provided an answer.

Part I: Influences

The crucial factor in most respondents' initial involvement in the scholarship of teaching and learning was the desire to explore questions about their students' learning. Only 3 percent reported this as "not important" and 81 percent described it as "very important" to their initial involvement. Almost as important to respondents were (a) a desire to pursue teaching and learning interests with new colleagues (only 6 percent deemed this "not important"); (b) connecting their interests to a recognized body of research (only 9 percent marked this "not important"); and (c) a desire to be part of the larger "movement" to bring greater recognition and reward to the scholarly work of teaching (10.5 percent marked this "not important"). (See Table A.1.)

Part II: Participation

With the exception of receiving external project funding, over half the respondents have participated in a full range of activities commonly associated with the scholarship of teaching and learning. (See Table A.2.) Over 85 percent of respondents reported:

- Framing and investigating teaching and learning questions inside their own classrooms (98 percent)
- Currently working on a project in the scholarship of teaching and learning (89 percent)
- Working with colleagues at their institution in framing and investigating questions about teaching and learning (88 percent)
- Working with colleagues beyond their institution (86 percent)

Part III: Consequences

Respondents reported that their involvement in the scholarship of teaching and learning has affected their work in a variety of ways, especially in the classroom, where it has led to changes in course design, assessment, and expectations for student learning. (See Table A.3.)

Questions about the impact of the scholarship of teaching and learning on professional advancement (promotion, tenure, hiring, and so on) are harder to interpret. Such questions were not applicable for many of these scholars because they were already at the highest professorial rank, or not seeking a new position. Nevertheless, among those who submitted scholarship of teaching and learning as part of their portfolios, most believe that it ultimately *strengthened* their case (whether in hiring, tenure, or promotion). And although some respondents reported being *unsure* what role it played in tenure (8 percent unsure) or in their most recent merit raise (25 percent unsure), very few reported that their submission of scholarship of teaching and learning *weakened* their cases (1 percent in reference to tenure; 2 percent in reference to merit raise). (See Table A.4.)

Part IV: Departmental Context

Respondents report a low level of departmental support for the scholarship of teaching and learning: 78 percent said that their departments do not offer adequate release time, and 74 percent indicated that their departments do not offer adequate financial support.

At the same time, in response to the statement "other departments provide more support for scholarship of teaching and learning involvement than my department does," 65 percent disagreed—suggesting that although support in their own departments could be stronger, it is similar to or better than that offered in other departments at the same institution.

Furthermore, around half of those surveyed indicated that their departments *do* provide some support for their scholarship in teaching and learning, noting that departmental policies encourage faculty to reflect on their teaching practices (58 percent), and that the department chair has actively encouraged involvement in the scholarship of teaching and learning (52 percent). (See Table A.5.)

Part V: Campus Context

Responses to questions in this section on campus context are consistent with those in the previous section focused on the department: approximately half of the respondents describe a climate where there is some support for the scholarship of teaching and learning. Many report shifts in campus policy and practice that suggest that support is on the rise—for instance, through new criteria for the evaluation of teaching and the establishment of structures to support the scholarship of teaching and learning. But when it comes to crucial aspects of time and money, a clear majority indicates insufficient support. And only 27 percent of respondents agreed that "support for the scholarship of teaching and learning at my institution is widespread." (See Table A.6.)

Part VI: Trends in Field of Study

A majority of respondents indicated that, in their field of study, they have witnessed change in scholarship of teaching and learning articles in the top journals, in journals devoted to teaching and learning, and in conference sessions on the scholarship of teaching. However, respondents tended to cite an increase in quantity rather than quality for top journal articles and conference sessions (7 percent and 9 percent reported increased quality for articles and conference sessions, respectively). When these responses were broken down according to field of study (arts and humanities, math and sciences, social sciences), no significant differences in response patterns emerged. (See Table A.7.)

Part VII: Support

A majority of respondents noted that participation in a national program or initiative to advance teaching and learning has been both available and important to their involvement in the scholarship of teaching and learning (31 percent marked "somewhat important," 60 percent marked "very important"). A majority of respondents (57 percent) also noted that release time is not available to them, nor do current tenure and promotion policies encourage the scholarship of teaching and learning (54 percent marked "not present").

On every question, the majority of respondents who noted the item's presence (availability) also indicated its importance to their work—suggesting that scholars benefit from a range of support structures and resources. (See Table A.8.)

Part VIII: Constraints

A majority of respondents agreed that the demands of research, confusion about the scholarship of teaching and learning, lack of leadership, and faculty concern about the potential increase in their workload all function as constraints to wider faculty participation. In a separate question asking respondents to identify the largest constraint, the research-teaching tension earned the most votes (35 percent). Other top picks were lack of time-money (24 percent), lack of leadership (12 percent), and confusion about what constitutes the scholarship of teaching and learning (8 percent).

Although 35 percent of respondents noted that faculty concern about academic freedom serves as a constraint, no one selected this item as the top obstacle to greater faculty involvement. (See Table A.9.)

Part IX: Predictions

Respondents tended to be positive in their predictions for the future. A majority (56 percent) believed that the scholarship of teaching and learning will be a respected specialty in their discipline within the decade, and 77 percent think it will be "fully counted" at their institution in the next twenty years. Most notably, perhaps, 98 percent believe that it will eventually contribute to widespread change in the nature of postsecondary learning, with 50 percent contending that the change will occur in the next five to ten years.

On a slightly less optimistic note, although a majority does not believe that the scholarship of teaching and learning will become a form of accountability used against faculty (56 percent), 17 percent do fear that it will happen in the next decade. (See Table A.10.)

Table A.1. Reasons for Involvement in the Scholarship of Teaching and Learning

	Percent of Respondents		
	Not Important	Somewhat Important	Very Important
I had questions about my students' learning that I wanted to explore.	3	16	81
I wanted to expand the range of scholarly work in which I am involved.	26	35	39
I wanted to connect my interests in teaching and learning to a recognized body of research.	9	42	50
I wanted to participate in the movement to bring greater recognition and reward to the scholarly work of teaching.	10.5	34.5	54
I wanted to find new colleagues with whom to pursue my interests in teaching and learning.	6	42	52
I was urged to become involved by colleagues who knew about the scholarship of teaching and learning.	48	25.5	26.5

Source: *Cox, Huber, and Hutchings, Survey of CASTL Scholars, 2004.*

Table A.2. Engagement in Scholarship of Teaching and Learning Activities

Engagement in Activities	Percent of Respondents	
	No	Yes
I have framed and investigated questions about teaching and learning within my own classroom.	2	98
I have worked with colleagues at my institution in framing and investigating questions about teaching and learning.	12	88
I have worked with colleagues beyond my institution in framing and investigating questions of shared concern about teaching and learning.	14	86
I have participated in campus-based professional development centered on the scholarship of teaching and learning.	19	81
I have attended a session devoted to the scholarship of teaching and learning at a discipline-based conference.	20	79
I have presented my scholarship on teaching and learning at a discipline-based conference.	17	82
My scholarship on teaching and learning has been published (or accepted for publication) in a journal or a book.	33	67
I have made my scholarship of teaching and learning available on a Web site.	43	57
I have received campus funding for a project on the scholarship of teaching and learning (other than funding for my CASTL participation).	49	50
I have received external funding for a project on the scholarship of teaching and learning (other than funding for my CASTL participation).	61	39
I have taken on a leadership role in changing (or trying to change) departmental policies on teaching to more fully reflect the principles of the scholarship of teaching and learning.	30	69
I have taken on a leadership role in changing (or trying to change) my institution's policies on teaching to more fully reflect the principles of the scholarship of teaching and learning.	31	68
I am currently working on a project in the scholarship of teaching and learning.	11	89

Source: *Cox, Huber, and Hutchings, Survey of CASTL Scholars, 2004.*

Table A.3. Consequences of Involvement in the Scholarship of Teaching and Learning

	Percent of Respondents			
Statement of Consequence	Strongly Disagree	Disagree	Agree	Strongly Agree
I have changed the design of my courses since becoming involved in the scholarship of teaching and learning.	0	6	35	58
I have changed the kinds of assessments I use in my courses as a result of my participation in the scholarship of teaching and learning.	0	8	40	52
Becoming involved in the scholarship of teaching and learning has contributed to my excitement about teaching.	0	2	25	73
My expectations for my own teaching have changed since participating in the scholarship of teaching and learning.	2	7	29	58
My expectations for my students' learning have changed since participating in the scholarship of teaching and learning.	0	8	32	60
The quality of my students' learning has changed since my involvement in the scholarship of teaching and learning.	0	8	56	31
I have documented improvements in my students' learning since becoming involved in the scholarship of teaching and learning.	1	15	52	29
More of my students achieve high standards of work since I became involved in the scholarship of teaching and learning.	1	20	49	20

Statement of Consequence	Percent of Respondents			
	Strongly Disagree	Disagree	Agree	Strongly Agree
I have found new colleagues and communities outside of CASTL for work on teaching and learning since participating in the scholarship of teaching and learning.	3	25	48	24
My work in the scholarship of teaching and learning has had a positive influence on teaching in my department beyond my own practice.	3	25	48	24
My involvement in the scholarship of teaching and learning is visible to my departmental colleagues.	2	13	47	35
My work in the scholarship of teaching and learning has influenced colleagues at my institution outside of my department.	3	15	50	30
I was recruited for a new position based on my scholarship of teaching and learning.	28	29	19	18
My participation in the scholarship of teaching and learning has opened up a major new career focus for me.	2	26	39	32
My participation in the scholarship of teaching and learning has opened up new opportunities for me at my institution.	3	27	46	21
My involvement in the scholarship of teaching and learning has heightened my interest in reading research on teaching and learning.	0	3	44	52

Source: *Cox, Huber, and Hutchings, Survey of CASTL Scholars, 2004.*

Table A.4. Role of the Scholarship of Teaching and Learning in Advancing Careers

	Percent of Respondents				
	Not Submitted	Submitted—Unsure of Role Played	Submitted—Weakened My Case	Submitted—Strengthened My Case	NA
In my most recent hiring	11	7	0	20	63
In my tenure case	7	8	1	25	58
In my promotion to full professor	3	8	0	19	71
In my most recent merit raise	4	25	2	40	29
In my most recent posttenure review	4	10	0	26	60

Source: *Cox, Huber, and Hutchings, Survey of CASTL Scholars, 2004.*

Table A.5. Departmental Support for the Scholarship of Teaching and Learning

Trend	Percent of Respondents: Strongly Disagree	Disagree	Agree	Strongly Agree
Over the past five years, my department has broadened the criteria for assessing teaching performance to more fully reflect the principles of the scholarship of teaching and learning.	14	43	32	7
My department's policies encourage faculty to reflect on their teaching practices.	10	30	42	16
In my department, other faculty members are actively involved in the scholarship of teaching and learning.	10	36	35	19
My department offers adequate release time to faculty who engage in the scholarship of teaching and learning.	43	35	18	3
My department provides adequate financialsupport for faculty to engage in the scholarship of teaching and learning.	38	36	20	4
Department norms encourage participationin the scholarship of teaching and learning.	20	39	25	12
Some of my departmental colleagues findmy work in the scholarship of teaching and learning problematic.	16	40	32	9
Faculty members in other departments atmy institution are actively involved in the scholarship of teaching and learning.	0	16	61	20
Other departments provide more supportfor scholarship of teaching and learning involvement than my department does.	15	50	18	7
When hiring new faculty, my department regards applicants' interest in the scholarship of teaching and learning favorably.	14	30	36	12
My department chair has actively encouraged involvement in the scholarship of teaching and learning.	15	27	36	16

Source: *Cox, Huber, and Hutchings, Survey of CASTL Scholars, 2004.*

Table A.6. Institutional Support for the Scholarship of Teaching and Learning

	Percent of Respondents			
Trend	Strongly Disagree	Disagree	Agree	Strongly Agree
Over the past five years, my institution has reexamined its approach to rewarding teaching.	8	27	48	15
Over the past five years, my institution has broadened the criteria for assessing teaching performance to reflect more fully the principles of the scholarship of teaching and learning.	10	35	43	9
Over the past five years, my institution has established formal structures to support the scholarship of teaching and learning.	9	27	43	20
Top-level academic leaders at my institution have taken significant steps to support the scholarship of teaching and learning.	12	32	38	16
Faculty members in formal leadership roles (senate president, department chair, and so on) have actively supported the scholarship of teaching and learning.	9	35	47	6
Support for the scholarship of teaching and learning at my institution is widespread.	11	58	23	4
The criteria for promotion decisions at my institution reflect the principles of the scholarship of teaching and learning.	15	42	30	4
The scholarship of teaching and learning is integrated into other institution priorities and initiatives.	9	39	43	4

Trend	Percent of Respondents			
	Strongly Disagree	Disagree	Agree	Strongly Agree
The criteria for tenure decisions at my institution reflect the principles of the scholarship of teaching and learning.	15	42	31	4
Faculty members at my institution have received tenure based at least in part on the scholarship of teaching and learning.	12	28	44	5
The criteria for the teaching awards presented at my institution are consistent with principles of the scholarship of teaching and learning.	11	35	42	7
There are adequate campus-level funding opportunities for scholarship of teaching and learning projects at my institution.	20	43	27	5
My institution offers adequate release time for the scholarship of teaching and learning.	28	48	1	2

Source: *Cox, Huber, and Hutchings, Survey of CASTL Scholars, 2004.*

Table A.7. Changes in Number and Quality of Journals, Articles, and Conference Sessions

	Percent of Respondents			
Changes Seen Over Past Five Years	**No Change**	**Increase in Number**	**Higher Standards**	**Not Sure**
Journals devoted to teaching and learning in my field of study.	45	20	15	7
Articles on the scholarship of teaching and learning in the top journals of my field.	38	29	7	12
Sessions about the scholarship of teaching and learning at the primary annual conference for my field.	19	42	9	13

Source: *Cox, Huber, and Hutchings, Survey of CASTL Scholars, 2004.*

Table A.8. Sources of Support That Advance Involvement in the Scholarship of Teaching and Learning

	Percent of Respondents			
	Not Present	Present but Unimportant to My Work	Present and Somewhat Important to My Work	Present and Very Important to My Work
Participation in a national program or initiative to advance teaching and learning (does not have to be limited to the scholarship of teaching and learning).	4	4	31	60
Supportive attitudes of departmental colleagues.	25	17	36	18
Release time from regular duties.	57	5	13	23
Campus funding for projects focused on teaching and learning.	35	17	29	19
Funding from external sources for projects focused on teaching and learning.	41	12	23	24
Tenure and promotion policies that encourage the scholarship of teaching and learning.	54	20	20	6
Professional development activities at my campus that focus on the scholarship of teaching and learning.	17	18	39	24
Efforts of professional associations to encourage the scholarship of teaching and learning.	11	21	41	25

Source: *Cox, Huber, and Hutchings, Survey of CASTL Scholars, 2004.*

Table A.9. Constraints on Greater Faculty Involvement in the Scholarship of Teaching and Learning

Trend	Percent of Respondents			
	Strongly Disagree	Disagree	Agree	Strongly Agree
The tension between demands for research productivity and the scholarship of teaching and learning is an obstacle to greater faculty involvement in the scholarship of teaching and learning at my institution. *(35% named this the single biggest obstacle.)*	5	15	33	46
Confusion among faculty about what constitutes the scholarship of teaching and learning is an obstacle to greater faculty involvement in the scholarship of teaching and learning at my institution. *(8% named this the single biggest obstacle.)*	2	8	63	27
Lack of leadership among top-level administrators is an obstacle to greater faculty involvement in the scholarship of teaching and learning at my institution. *(12% named this the single biggest obstacle.)*	7	20	41	28
Many faculty members' perception of the scholarship of teaching and learning as an addition to their workload is an obstacle to greater faculty involvement in the scholarship of teaching and learning at my institution. *(10% named this the single biggest obstacle.)*	2	12	49	32
The fear that making teaching public could undermine faculty members' academic freedom is an obstacle to greater faculty involvement in the scholarship of teaching and learning at my institution. *(0% named this the single biggest obstacle.)*	17	43	30	5

Other answers: *24% said the biggest obstacle was lack of time and/or money. Another 3% named other constraints like inertia or problems of reform sustainability.*

Source: *Cox, Huber, and Hutchings, Survey of CASTL Scholars, 2004.*

Table A.10. Predictions for the Future of the Scholarship of Teaching and Learning

	Percent of Respondents			
	5–10 Years	10–20 Years	20+ Years	Never
It will become a fully legitimate, "counted" kind of scholarly work on my campus.	45	32	5	11
It will become a respected specialty in my discipline or professional field.	56	26	4	9
It will become an expectation of all faculty at various points in their careers, institutionalized through campus policies.	17	26	10	44
It will contribute to widespread changes in how students learn in postsecondary classrooms.	50	32	12	2
It will disappear and leave no trace.	2	0	0	91
It will become a form of accountability used against faculty.	17	9	3	56

Source: *Cox, Huber, and Hutchings, Survey of CASTL Scholars, 2004.*

REFERENCES

Albert, L. S., Moore, M. R., and Mincey, K. C. "An Ongoing Journey." In B. Cambridge (ed.), *Campus Progress: Supporting the Scholarship of Teaching and Learning*. Washington, D.C.: American Association for Higher Education, 2004.

Alexander, P. "The Development of Expertise: The Journey from Acclimation to Proficiency." *Educational Researcher,* Nov. 2003, *32*(8), 10–14.

Anderson, G. L., and Herr, K. "The New Paradigm Wars: Is There Room for Rigorous Practitioner Knowledge in Schools and Universities?" *Educational Researcher,* June-July 1999, *28*(5), 12–21, 40.

Angelo, T. A., and Cross, K. P. *Classroom Assessment Techniques: A Handbook for College Teachers* (2nd ed.). San Francisco: Jossey-Bass, 1993.

Ashton-Warner, S. *Teacher.* New York: Simon & Schuster, 1963.

Association of American Colleges and Universities. *Greater Expectations: A New Vision for Learning as a Nation Goes to College.* Washington, D.C.: Association of American Colleges and Universities, 2002. http://www.greaterexpectations.org/. Accessed April 6, 2005.

Association of American Colleges and Universities. "Evaluating Students' Best Work: SIUE Embeds Assessment in Capstone Learning Projects." *AAC&U News,* Sept. 2004, (31), 1–3. http://www.aacu-edu.org/aacu_news/AACUNews04/September04/feature.cfm. Accessed April 6, 2005.

Astin, A., Korn, W., and Dey, E. *The American College Teacher: National Norms for the 1989–90 HERI Faculty Survey.* Los Angeles: Higher Education Research Institute, University of California, 1991.

Austin, R. D. "Managing Knowledge Workers: Evolving Practices and Trends." *Science: Next Wave,* Apr. 26, 2002. http://nextwave.sciencemag.org/cgi/content/full/2002/04/25/5? Accessed April 6, 2005.

Axelrod, J. *Teaching by Discussion in the College Program: Report of a Study.* Chicago: University of Chicago Press, 1949.

Ayers, E. L. "Doing Scholarship on the Web: 10 Years of Triumphs—and a Disappointment." *Chronicle of Higher Education,* Jan. 30, 2004, *50*(21), B24–25.

Babb, M. "Looking at Impact: Documenting the Scholarship of Teaching and Learning on Campus." Unpublished paper. Menlo Park, Calif.: The Carnegie Foundation for the Advancement of Teaching, 2003.

Bailyn, B. *Education in the Forming of American Society.* New York: Vintage Books, 1960.

Baker, P. J. "The Helter-Skelter Relationship Between Teaching and Research: A Cluster of Problems and Small Wins." *Teaching Sociology,* Jan. 1986, *14*(1), 50–66.

Baker, P. J., and Zey-Ferrell, M. "Local and Cosmopolitan Orientations of Faculty." *Teaching Sociology,* 1984, *12*(1), 82–106.

Barnes, L. B., Christensen, C. R, and Hansen, A. J. *Teaching and the Case Method: Text, Cases, and Readings.* Boston: Harvard Business School Press, 1994.

Barzun, J. *Teacher in America.* Lanham, Mass.: University Press of America, 1986. (Originally published 1945)

Bass, H. "Developing Scholars and Professionals: The Case of Mathematics." In C. Golde and G. Walker (eds.), *Envisioning the Future of Doctoral Education: Preparing Stewards of the Discipline.* San Francisco: Jossey-Bass, 2006.

Bass, R. "The Role of the Student on a Committee for Academic Reform." *Liberal Education,* Summer 1981, *67*(2), 125–128.

Bass, R. "Crossroads: The Release Version." *American Studies Association Newsletter,* Sept. 1995. http://www.georgetown.edu/crossroads/AmericanStudiesAssn/newsletter/archive/articles/xroads3.html. Accessed April 6, 2005.

Bass, R. "American Literary Traditions." Course portfolio, 1997a. http://www.georgetown.edu/bassr/traditions.html. Accessed April 6, 2005.

Bass, R. "Engines of Inquiry: Teaching, Technology, and Learner-Centered Approaches to Culture and History." In R. Bass (ed.), *Engines of Inquiry: A Practical Guide for Using Technology in Teaching American Culture.* Washington, D.C.: American Studies Crossroads Project, American Studies Association, 1997b. http://www.georgetown.edu/crossroads/guide/engines.html. Accessed April 6, 2005.

Bass, R. Final oral report. Carnegie Academy for the Scholarship of Teaching and Learning (CASTL). Menlo Park, Calif.: The Carnegie Foundation for the Advancement of Teaching, June 1999a.

Bass, R. "The Scholarship of Teaching: What's the Problem?" *Inventio: Creative Thinking About Learning and Teaching,* Feb. 1999b, *1*(1). http://www.doit.gmu.edu/Archives/feb98/randybass.htm. Accessed April 6, 2005.

Bass, R. "Seeing Teaching and Learning in Time." Oral presentation by Randy Bass to the 2003–04 CASTL Scholars at The Carnegie Foundation for the Advancement of Teaching, Stanford, Calif., June 21, 2004.

Batson, T., and Bass, R. "Primacy of Process: Teaching and Learning in the Computer Age." *Change,* Mar.-Apr. 1996, *28*(2), 42–47.

Becher, T., and Trowler, P. R. *Academic Tribes and Territories: Intellectual Enquiry and the Culture of Disciplines* (2nd ed.). Buckingham, U.K.: Society for Research into Higher Education and Open University Press, 2001.

Bender, E., and Gray, D. "The Scholarship of Teaching and Learning." *Research and Creative Activity,* Apr. 1999, *22*(1), 3–5.

Bender, T., and Schorske, C. E. (eds.). *American Academic Culture in Transformation: Fifty Years, Four Disciplines.* Princeton, N.J.: American Academy of Arts and Sciences, 1997.

Bennett, C. "My Course Portfolio: A Window on Student Learning and an Entrance into Further Study." Paper presented at the Conference on Disciplinary Styles in the Scholarship of Teaching and Learning, Rockhurst University, Kansas City, Mo., Apr. 19, 2002. http://knowledge.carnegiefoundation.org/icons/conversions/Rockhurst%20paper.doc.htm. Accessed April 6, 2005.

Bennett, C., and Dewar, J. "June Presentation." Carnegie Academy for the Scholarship of Teaching and Learning (CASTL) Electronic Workspace. Stanford, Calif.: The Carnegie Foundation for the Advancement of Teaching, June 2004a. http://myweb.lmu.edu/carnegie/june_5_20_04. Accessed April 6, 2005.

Bennett, C., and Dewar, J. "What You Ought to Know About Collaboration on a SoTL Project." *National Teaching and Learning Forum,* Dec. 2004b, *14*(1), 4–6. http://cstl.syr.edu/Cstl/NTLF/v14n1/carnegie.htm. Accessed April 6, 2005.

Benson, S. A. "Defining the Scholarship of Teaching in Microbiology Education." *Focus on Microbiology Education,* Spring 2001a, *7*(3), 1–6.

Benson, S. A. "Greetings from Spencer Benson." Carnegie Academy for the Scholarship of Teaching and Learning (CASTL) listserv. CASTL Electronic Workspace. Stanford, Calif.: The Carnegie Foundation for the Advancement of Teaching, Apr. 16, 2001b.

Bernstein, D. J. "A Departmental System for Balancing the Development and Evaluation of College Teaching: A Commentary on Cavanagh." *Innovative Higher Education,* Spring 1996, *20*(4), 241–248.

Bernstein, D. J. "Putting the Focus on Student Learning." In P. Hutchings (ed.), *The Course Portfolio: How Faculty Can Examine Their Teaching to Advance Practice and Improve Student Learning.* Washington, D.C.: American Association for Higher Education, 1998.

Bernstein, D. J. "Bernstein Project Summary." *Peer Review of Teaching.* Lincoln, Nebr.: University of Nebraska, Lincoln, Jan. 2000. http://www.unl.edu/peerrev/examples/bernstein/index.html. Accessed April 6, 2005.

Bernstein, D. J. "Representing the Intellectual Work in Teaching Through Peer-Reviewed Course Portfolios." In S. Davis and W. Buskist (eds.), *The Teaching of Psychology: Essays in Honor of Wilbert J. McKeachie and Charles L. Brewer.* Hillsdale, N.J.: Erlbaum, 2001.

Bilimoria, D., and Fukami, C. "The Scholarship of Teaching and Learning in the Management Sciences: Disciplinary Style and Content." In M. T. Huber and S. P. Morreale (eds.), *Disciplinary Styles in the Scholarship of Teaching and Learning: Exploring Common Ground.* Washington, D.C.: American Association for Higher Education and The Carnegie Foundation for the Advancement of Teaching, 2002.

Bloom, B. S. *All Our Children Learning.* New York: McGraw-Hill, 1981.

Bloom, B. S., and Associates. *The Taxonomy of Educational Objectives: Cognitive Domain.* New York: David McKay, 1956.

Bollier, D. *Public Assets, Private Profits: Reclaiming the American Commons in an Age of Market Enclosure.* Washington, D.C.: New America Foundation, 2001.

Booth, W. C. *The Vocation of a Teacher: Rhetorical Occasions: 1967–1988.* Chicago: University of Chicago Press, 1988.

Bourdieu, P. *Outline of a Theory of Practice.* (R. Nice, trans.). Cambridge, UK: Cambridge University Press, 1977.

Boyer Commission on Educating Undergraduates in the Research University. *Reinventing Undergraduate Education: A Blueprint for America's Research Universities.* Stony Brook: State University of New York for The Carnegie Foundation for the Advancement of Teaching, 1998.

Boyer, E. *Scholarship Reconsidered: Priorities of the Professoriate.* Princeton, N.J.: The Carnegie Foundation for the Advancement of Teaching, 1990.

Boyer, E., and Levine, A. *A Quest for Common Learning: The Aims of General Education.* Princeton, N.J.: The Carnegie Foundation for the Advancement of Teaching, 1981.

Bransford, J. D., Brown, A. L., and Cocking, R. R. (eds.). *How People Learn: Brain, Mind, Experience, and School.* Washington, D.C.: National Research Council, Committee on Developments in the Science of Learning, National Academy Press, 1999.

Brew, A. *The Nature of Research: Inquiry in Academic Contexts.* London: Routledge Falmer, 2001.

Brew, A. "Teaching and Research: New Relationships and Their Implications for Inquiry-Based Teaching and Learning in Higher Education." *Higher Education Research and Development,* 2003, 22(1), 3–17.

Broder, J. M., and Kalivoda, P. L. "A Freestanding Teaching Academy." In B. Cambridge (ed.), *Campus Progress: Supporting the Scholarship of*

Teaching and Learning. Washington, D.C.: American Association for Higher Education, 2004.

Brookfield, S. D. *Understanding and Facilitating Adult Learning: A Comprehensive Analysis of Principles and Effective Practices*. San Francisco: Jossey-Bass, 1986.

Brookfield, S. D. *Becoming a Critically Reflective Teacher*. San Francisco: Jossey-Bass, 1995.

Brooks, C., and Brogan, T.V.F. "The New Criticism." In A. Preminger, T.V.F. Brogan, and F. J. Warnke (eds.), *The New Princeton Encyclopedia of Poetry and Poetics*. Princeton, N.J.: Princeton University Press, 1993.

Brown, J. S. "Growing Up Digital: How the Web Changes Work, Education, and the Ways People Learn." *Change,* Mar.-Apr. 2000, *32*(2), 10–21.

Brown, J. S., and Duguid, P. *The Social Life of Information*. Boston: Harvard Business School Press, 2000.

Calder, L. "Looking for Learning in the History Survey." *American Historical Perspectives,* Mar. 2002, *40*(3), 43–45.

Calder, L., Cutler, W. W. III, and Kelly, T. M. "History Lessons: Historians and the Scholarship of Teaching and Learning." In M. T. Huber and S. P. Morreale (eds.), *Disciplinary Styles in the Scholarship of Teaching and Learning: Exploring Common Ground*. Washington, D.C.: American Association for Higher Education and The Carnegie Foundation for the Advancement of Teaching, 2002.

Caldwell, I., and Thomason, D. *The Rule of Four*. New York: Dial Press, 2004.

California State University-Monterey Bay. "Our Vision Statement," Sept. 27, 1994. http://csumb.edu/vision. Accessed April 6, 2005.

Cambridge, B. L. (ed.). *Electronic Portfolios: Emerging Practices in Student, Faculty, and Institutional Learning*. Washington, D.C.: American Association for Higher Education, 2001.

Cambridge, B. L. (ed.). *Campus Progress: Supporting the Scholarship of Teaching and Learning*. Washington, D.C.: American Association for Higher Education, 2004.

Cambridge, B. L., and Williams, A. C. *Portfolio Learning*. Upper Saddle River, N.J.: Prentice Hall, 1998.

Carnegie Council on Policy Studies in Higher Education. *Three Thousand Futures: The Next Twenty Years for Higher Education*. San Francisco: Jossey-Bass, 1980.

Carroll, J. B. "A Model of School Learning." *Teachers College Record,* May 1963, *64*(8), 723–733.

Center for the Advancement of Engineering Education. "CAEE Overview," n.d. http://www.engr.washington.edu/caee. Accessed April 6, 2005.

Center for the Integration of Research, Teaching, and Learning. "Our Work: Overview," n.d. http://cirtl.wceruw.org/ourwork_overview.html. Accessed April 6, 2005.

Centre for Higher Education Research & Information. *Ten Years On: Changing Higher Education in a Changing World.* London: Centre for Higher Education Research & Information, Open University, 2004. http://www.open.ac.uk/cheri/ten_years_on1.htm. Accessed April 6, 2005.

Centra, J. A. *Reflective Faculty Evaluation: Enhancing Teaching and Determining Faculty Effectiveness.* San Francisco: Jossey-Bass, 1993.

Cerbin, W. "Investigating Student Learning in a Problem-Based Psychology Course." In P. Hutchings (ed.), *Opening Lines: Approaches to the Scholarship of Teaching and Learning.* Menlo Park, Calif.: The Carnegie Foundation for the Advancement of Teaching, 2000.

Choy, S. *Nontraditional Undergraduates* (NCES 2002–012). Washington, D.C.: United States Department of Education, National Center for Education Statistics, 2002.

Christensen, C. M. *The Innovator's Dilemma.* New York: HarperBusiness, 2003.

Christensen, C. M., and Raynor, M. E. *The Innovator's Solution: Creating and Sustaining Successful Growth.* Boston: Harvard Business School Press, 2003.

Christensen, C. R., Garvin, D. A., and Sweet, A. (eds.). *Education for Judgment: The Artistry of Discussion Leadership.* Boston: Harvard Business School Press, 1991.

Ciccone, A. "Furthering the Scholarship of Teaching and Learning the Wisconsin Way." In B. Cambridge (ed.), *Campus Progress: Supporting the Scholarship of Teaching and Learning.* Washington, D.C.: American Association for Higher Education, 2004.

Cochran-Smith, M., and Lytle, S. "The Teacher Research Movement: A Decade Later." *Educational Researcher,* Oct. 1999, *28*(7), 15–25.

Colby, A., Ehrlich, T., Beaumont, E., and Stephens, J. *Educating Citizens: Preparing America's Undergraduates for Lives of Moral and Civic Responsibility.* San Francisco: Jossey-Bass, 2003.

Collins, A., Brown, J. S., and Holum, A. "Cognitive Apprenticeship: Making Thinking Visible." *American Educator,* Winter 1991, *15*(3), 6–12, 38–47.

Cooperstein, B. "Learning to Think Mathematically: Introduction to Problem Solving Course Portfolio." Electronic course portfolio. 2000. http://gallery.carnegiefoundation.org/bcooperstein/. Accessed October 7, 2003.

Coppola, B. P., Daniels, D. S., and Pontrello, J. K. "Using Structured Study Groups to Create Chemistry Honors Sections." In J. E. Miller, M. S. Miller, and J. E. Groccia (eds.), *Student-Assisted Teaching: A Guide to Student-Faculty Teamwork.* Bolton, Mass.: Anker, 2001.

Coppola, B. P., Ege, S. N., and Lawton, R. G. "The University of Michigan Undergraduate Chemistry Curriculum 2. Instructional Strategies and Assessment." *Journal of Chemical Education,* Jan. 1997, *74*(1), 84–94.

Coppola, B. P., and Jacobs, D. C. "Is the Scholarship of Teaching and Learning New to Chemistry?" In M. T. Huber and S. P. Morreale (eds.), *Disciplinary Styles in the Scholarship of Teaching and Learning: Exploring Common Ground.* Washington, D.C.: American Association for Higher Education and The Carnegie Foundation for the Advancement of Teaching, 2002.

Corrada, R. Final oral report. Carnegie Academy for the Scholarship of Teaching and Learning (CASTL). Menlo Park, Calif.: The Carnegie Foundation for the Advancement of Teaching, June 2001a.

Corrada, R. "Using Technology to Support Active Learning in a Labor Law Classroom." In O. V. Burton (ed.), *Wayfarer: Charting Advances in Social Sciences and Humanities Computing* (CD-ROM). Champaign: University of Illinois Press, 2001b.

Corrada, R. "Making the Case: Retention, Tenure, and Promotion, and the Scholarship of Teaching and Learning." Presentation by Roberto Corrada at the Annual Meeting of the Association of American Colleges and Universities, Washington, D.C., Jan. 23, 2004.

Coulter, D. "The Epic and the Novel: Dialogism and Teacher Research." *Educational Researcher,* Apr. 1999, *18*(3), 4–13.

Cox, R., Huber, M. T., and Hutchings, P. *Survey of CASTL Scholars.* Stanford, Calif.: The Carnegie Foundation for the Advancement of Teaching, 2004.

Crane, D. *Invisible Colleges: Diffusion of Knowledge in Scientific Communities.* Chicago: University of Chicago Press, 1972.

Cross, K. P. "What Do We Know About Student Learning and How Do We Know It?" Keynote address at the American Association for Higher Education National Conference on Higher Education, Washington, D.C., Mar. 1998.

Cross, K. P., and Steadman, M. *Classroom Research: Implementing the Scholarship of Teaching.* San Francisco: Jossey-Bass, 1996.

Cuban, L. *How Scholars Trumped Teachers: Change Without Reform in University Curriculum, Teaching, and Research, 1890–1990.* New York: Teachers College Press, 1999.

Damasio, A. *Descartes' Error: Emotion, Reason, and the Human Brain.* New York: Putnam, 1994.

Diamond, R. M. *Aligning Faculty Rewards with Institutional Mission: Statements, Policies, and Guidelines.* Bolton, Mass.: Anker, 1999.

Donald, J. G. *Learning to Think: Disciplinary Perspectives.* San Francisco: Jossey-Bass, 2002.

Downey, G. L., Dumit, J., and Traweek, S. "Corridor Talk." In G. L. Downey and J. Dumit (eds.), *Cyborgs and Citadels: Anthropological Interventions in Emerging Sciences and Technologies.* Santa Fe, N.M.: School of American Research Press, 1997.

Duffy, D. K. "Resilient Students, Resilient Communities." In P. Hutchings (ed.), *Opening Lines: Approaches to the Scholarship of Teaching and Learning.* Menlo Park, Calif.: The Carnegie Foundation for the Advancement of Teaching, 2000.

Eagleton, T. "Company Man." (Book review of *The Age of Shakespeare,* by F. Kermode). *The Nation,* Mar. 1, 2004, *278*(8), 29–32.

Eble, K. E. *The Craft of Teaching: A Guide to Mastering the Professor's Art.* San Francisco: Jossey-Bass, 1988.

Edgerton, R., Hutchings, P., and Quinlan, K. *The Teaching Portfolio: Capturing the Scholarship in Teaching.* Washington, D.C.: American Association for Higher Education, 1991.

Ege, S. N., Coppola, B. P., and Lawton, R. G. "The University of Michigan Undergraduate Chemistry Curriculum 1. Philosophy, Curriculum, and the Nature of Change." *Journal of Chemical Education,* Jan. 1997, *74*(1), 74–83.

Ehrmann, S. C. "The Scholarship of Teaching—Step One." Flashlight Program, Part II. June 16, 2002. http://www.tltgroup.org/resources/Flashlight/Scholarship_What-2.html. Accessed April 6, 2005.

Eisner, E. "Aesthetic Modes of Knowing." In E. Eisner (ed.), *Learning and Teaching the Ways of Knowing: Eighty-Fourth Yearbook of the National Society for the Study of Education.* Chicago: University of Chicago Press, 1985.

Ellis, R. *SLA Research and Language Teaching.* Oxford, U.K.: Oxford University Press, 1997.

Elmendorf, H. "Conversational Biologists—Disciplinary Inroads Through Discourse." Final oral report. The Carnegie Academy for the Scholarship of Teaching and Learning (CASTL). Stanford, Calif.: The Carnegie Foundation for the Advancement of Teaching, June 2004.

Elton, L. "Research and Teaching: Conditions for a Positive Link." *Teaching in Higher Education,* Jan. 2001, *6*(1), 43–56.

Erskine, J. *My Life as a Teacher.* Philadelphia: Lippincott, 1948.

Fallon, D. "On the Past, Present, and Future of the Liberal Arts." Paper presented by Daniel Fallon at the Cornell Conference on the Idea of a University, Ithaca, N.Y., Oct. 18, 2002.

Feito, J. "Follow-Up Questionnaire." The Carnegie Academy for the Scholarship of Teaching and Learning (CASTL) Electronic Workspace. Menlo Park, Calif.: The Carnegie Foundation for the Advancement of Teaching, Oct. 2001a.

Feito, J. "Project Update." The Carnegie Academy for the Scholarship of Teaching and Learning (CASTL) Electronic Workspace. Menlo Park, Calif.: The Carnegie Foundation for the Advancement of Teaching, Oct. 15, 2001b.

Feito, J. "Exploring Intellectual Community: Group Learning Processes in Traditional 'Great Books' Seminars." Carnegie Academy for the Scholarship of Teaching and Learning Final Report. CASTL Electronic Workspace. Menlo Park, Calif.: The Carnegie Foundation for the Advancement of Teaching, June 13, 2002.

Fenstermacher, G. D. "Some Considerations on the Redesign of General and Integrative Studies at Virginia Tech." Paper presented at Virginia Technological University, Blacksburg, Va., Mar. 28, 2003.

Fink, L. D. *Creating Significant Learning Experiences: An Integrated Approach to Designing College Courses.* San Francisco: Jossey-Bass, 2003.

Fink, L. D. "President's Column." *POD Network News,* Spring/Summer 2004, 1–2. http://www.podnetwork.org/publications&resources/newsletter/spring04.htm. Accessed April 6, 2005.

Finkel, D. L. *Teaching with Your Mouth Shut.* Portsmouth, N.H.: Boynton/Cook/Heinemann, 2000.

Flannery, M. "Teaching About Images of the Cell." Carnegie Academy for the Scholarship of Teaching and Learning (CASTL) project update. CASTL Electronic Workspace. Menlo Park, Calif.: The Carnegie Foundation for the Advancement of Teaching, Oct. 2000.

Flannery, M. Final oral report. Carnegie Academy for the Scholarship of Teaching and Learning (CASTL). Menlo Park, Calif.: The Carnegie Foundation for the Advancement of Teaching, June, 2001a.

Flannery, M. "The Mind-Body Problem." *American Biology Teacher,* Oct. 2001b, *62*(8), 610–615.

Flannery, M. "Thoughts on My Carnegie Project at the Halfway Point." Carnegie Academy for the Scholarship of Teaching and Learning (CASTL) interim report. CASTL Electronic Workspace. Menlo Park, Calif.: The Carnegie Foundation for the Advancement of Teaching, Jan. 2001c.

Foster, A. L. "Who Should Own Science? A Group Proposing Alternative Licenses Says Patents Thwart Research; Some Officials Disagree." *Chronicle of Higher Education,* Oct. 1, 2004, *LI*(6), A33.

Gadamer, H. *Philosophical Hermeneutics.* (D. E. Linge, trans. and ed.). Berkeley: University of California Press, 1976.

Gale, R. "The 'Magic' of Learning from Each Other." *Carnegie Perspectives,* Sept. 2004. http://www.carnegiefoundation.org/perspectives/perspectives2004.Sept.htm. Accessed April 6, 2005.

Gale, R., and Golde, C. "Doctoral Education and the Scholarship of Teaching and Learning." *Peer Review,* Spring 2004, *6*(3), 8–12.

Gallison, P. *Image and Logic: A Material Culture of Microphysics.* Chicago: University of Chicago Press, 1997.

Gardner, H. *Frames of Mind: The Theory of Multiple Intelligences.* New York: Basic Books, 1983.

Geertz, C. *Local Knowledge: Further Essays in Interpretive Anthropology.* New York: Basic Books, 1983.

Gibbons, M., and Associates. *The New Production of Knowledge: The Dynamics of Science and Research in Contemporary Societies.* Thousand Oaks, Calif.: Sage, 1994.

Giddens, A. "Living in a Post-Traditional Society." In U. Beck, A. Giddens, and S. Lash (eds.), *Reflexive Modernization: Politics, Tradition, and Aesthetics in the Modern Social Order.* Stanford, Calif.: Stanford University Press, 1994.

Glaser, R. "Education and Thinking: The Role of Knowledge." *American Psychologist,* 1984, *39*(2), 93–104.

Glassick, C. E., Huber, M. T., and Maeroff, G. I. *Scholarship Assessed: Evaluation of the Professoriate.* San Francisco: Jossey-Bass, 1997.

Gleason, P., and Klein, J. "Sustaining a Community of Practice at Middlesex College." In B. Cambridge (ed.), *Campus Progress: Supporting the Scholarship of Teaching and Learning.* Washington, D.C.: American Association for Higher Education, 2004.

Goldin, C. "The Human Capital Century and American Leadership: Virtues of the Past." *Journal of Economic History,* June 2001, *61*(2), 263–292.

Goleman, D. *Emotional Intelligence: Why It Can Matter More Than IQ.* New York: Bantam, 1995.

Graff, G. *Professing Literature: An Institutional History.* Chicago: University of Chicago Press, 1987.

Graff, G. *Clueless in Academe: How Schooling Obscures the Life of the Mind.* New Haven, Conn.: Yale University Press, 2003.

Greene, L. "Toward a Model of Student Questioning." Carnegie Academy for the Scholarship of Teaching and Learning (CASTL) Electronic Workspace. Stanford, Calif.: The Carnegie Foundation for the Advancement of Teaching, June 2004. http://kml2.carnegiefoundation.org/html/poster.php?id=512. Accessed April 6, 2005.

Grossman, P. L., Wilson, S. M., and Shulman, L. S. "Teachers of Substance: Subject Matter Knowledge for Teaching." In M. C. Reynolds (ed.), *Knowledge Base for the Beginning Teacher.* New York: Pergamon, 1989.

Guillory, J. "The Very Idea of Pedagogy." *Profession 2002,*164–171.

Gumport, P. J. *Academic Pathfinders: Knowledge Creation and Feminist Scholarship.* Westport, Conn.: Greenwood, 2002.

Gumport, P. J., and Zemsky, R. "Drawing New Maps for a Changing Enterprise." *Change,* July-Aug. 2003, *35*(4), 30–35.

Halpern, D. F., and Hakel, M. D. "Applying the Science of Learning to the University and Beyond: Teaching for Long-Term Retention and Transfer." *Change,* July-Aug. 2003, *35*(4), 36–41.

Harvard Committee. *General Education in a Free Society: Report of the Harvard Committee.* Cambridge, Mass.: Harvard University Press, 1945.

Hatch, T., Bass, R., Iiyoshi, T., and Pointer Mace, D. "Building Knowledge for Teaching and Learning: The Promise of Scholarship in a Networked Environment." *Change,* Sept.-Oct. 2004, *36*(5), 42–49.

Hattie, J., and Marsh, H. W. "The Relationship Between Research and Teaching: A Meta-Analysis." *Review of Educational Research,* Winter 1996, *66*(4), 507–542.

Healey, M. "Developing the Scholarship of Teaching in Higher Education: A Discipline-Based Approach." *Higher Education Research & Development,* July 2002, *19*(2), 169–189.

Highet, G. *The Art of Teaching.* New York: Knopf, 1950.

Holcomb, J. "The Ethics of Comparison: A Statistician Wrestles with the Orthodoxy of a Control Group." In P. Hutchings (ed.), *Ethics of Inquiry: Issues in the Scholarship of Teaching and Learning.* Menlo Park, Calif.: The Carnegie Foundation for the Advancement of Teaching, 2002.

Holton, G. *The Scientific Imagination.* New York: Cambridge University Press, 1978.

hooks, b. *Teaching to Transgress: Education as the Practice of Freedom.* New York: Routledge, 1994.

Horn, L., Peter, K., Rooney, K., and Malizio, A. G. *Profile of Undergraduates in U.S. Postsecondary Institutions: 1999–2000* (NCES 2002–168). Washington, D.C.: United States Department of Education, National Center for Education Statistics, 2002.

"How Can Colleges Prove They're Doing Their Jobs?" *Chronicle of Higher Education,* Sept. 3, 2004, *51*(2), B6.

Howery, C. "The Culture of Teaching in Sociology." In M. T. Huber and S. P. Morreale (eds.), *Disciplinary Styles in the Scholarship of Teaching and Learning: Exploring Common Ground.* Washington, D.C.: American Association for Higher Education and The Carnegie Foundation for the Advancement of Teaching, 2002.

Huber, M. T. *Community College Faculty: Attitudes and Trends, 1997.* Stanford, Calif.: National Center for Postsecondary Improvement, 1998.

Huber, M. T. "Developing Discourse Communities Around the Scholarship of Teaching." *National Teaching and Learning Forum* (supplemental material),

Oct. 1999, *8*(6), n.p. http://www.ntlf.com/html/lib/carnegie/86huber.htm. Accessed April 6, 2005.

Huber, M. T. "Disciplinary Styles in the Scholarship of Teaching: Reflections on The Carnegie Academy for the Scholarship of Teaching and Learning." In C. Rust (ed.), *Improving Student Learning: Improving Student Learning Through the Disciplines.* Oxford, U.K.: Oxford Brookes University, Oxford Centre for Staff and Learning Development, 2000.

Huber, M. T. "Faculty Evaluation and the Development of Academic Careers." In C. Colbeck (ed.), *Evaluating Faculty Performance. New Directions for Institutional Research* (pp. 73–83). San Francisco: Jossey-Bass, 2002.

Huber, M. T. *Balancing Acts: The Scholarship of Teaching and Learning in Academic Careers.* Washington, D.C.: American Association for Higher Education and The Carnegie Foundation for the Advancement of Teaching, 2004

Huber, M. T., and Cox, R. "Work That Matters Should Be Work That Counts." *Carnegie Perspectives,* Feb. 2004. http://www.carnegiefoundation.org/perspectives/perspectives2004.Feb.htm. Accessed April 6, 2005.

Huber, M. T., and Hutchings, P. *Integrative Learning: Mapping the Terrain.* Washington, D.C.: Association of American Colleges and Universities, 2005.

Huber, M. T., Hutchings, P., and Shulman, L. S. "The Scholarship of Teaching and Learning Today." In K. A. O'Meara and R. E. Rice (eds.), *Faculty Priorities Reconsidered: Rewarding Multiple Forms of Scholarship.* San Francisco: Jossey-Bass with the American Association for Higher Education, 2005.

Huber, M. T., and Morreale, S. P (eds.). *Disciplinary Styles in the Scholarship of Teaching and Learning: Exploring Common Ground.* Washington, D.C.: The American Association for Higher Education and The Carnegie Foundation for the Advancement of Teaching, 2002a.

Huber, M. T., and Morreale, S. P. "Situating the Scholarship of Teaching and Learning: A Cross-Disciplinary Conversation." In M. T. Huber and S. P. Morreale (eds.), *Disciplinary Styles in the Scholarship of Teaching and Learning: Exploring Common Ground.* Washington, D.C.: American Association for Higher Education and The Carnegie Foundation for the Advancement of Teaching, 2002b.

Hutchings, P. (ed.). *Making Teaching Community Property: A Menu for Peer Collaboration and Peer Review.* Washington, D.C.: American Association for Higher Education, 1996.

Hutchings, P. (ed.). *The Course Portfolio: How Faculty Can Examine Their Teaching to Advance Practice and Improve Student Learning.* Washington, D.C.: American Association for Higher Education, 1998.

Hutchings, P. "Approaching the Scholarship of Teaching and Learning." In P. Hutchings (ed.), *Opening Lines: Approaches to the Scholarship of Teaching and Learning.* Menlo Park, Calif.: The Carnegie Foundation for the Advancement of Teaching, 2000.

Hutchings, P. (ed.). *Ethics of Inquiry: Issues in the Scholarship of Teaching and Learning.* Menlo Park, Calif.: The Carnegie Foundation for the Advancement of Teaching, 2002.

Hutchings, P. "Building Pedagogical Intelligence." *Carnegie Perspectives,* Jan. 2005. http://www.carnegiefoundation.org/perspectives/perspectives2005.Jan.htm. Accessed April 6, 2005.

Hutchings, P., and Clarke, S. "The Scholarship of Teaching and Learning: Contributing to Reform in Graduate Education." In D. Wolfe, A. Austin, and Associates (eds.), *Paths to the Professoriate.* San Francisco: Jossey-Bass, 2004.

Hutchings, P., and Shulman, L. S. "The Scholarship of Teaching: New Elaborations, New Developments." *Change,* Sept.-Oct. 1999, *31*(5), 10–15.

Hutchinson, Y. D. "A Friend of Their Minds: Capitalizing on the Oral Tradition of My African American Students," 2003. http://gallery.carnegiefoundation.org/yhutchinson. Accessed April 6, 2005.

Iser, W. *The Act of Reading.* Baltimore: Johns Hopkins University Press, 1978.

Jacobs, D. "A Chemical Mixture of Methods." In P. Hutchings (ed.), *Opening Lines: Approaches to the Scholarship of Teaching and Learning.* Menlo Park, Calif.: The Carnegie Foundation for the Advancement of Teaching, 2000.

Jacobs, D. "An Alternative Approach to General Chemistry: Addressing the Needs of At-Risk Students with Cooperative Learning Strategies." Electronic course portfolio, 2001. http://kml2.carnegiefoundation.org/gallery/djacobs/index2.htm. Accessed April 18, 2004.

Jameson, J. "Setting a Scholarly Tone: Teaching Circles in the History Department at Kent State University." In P. Hutchings (ed.), *Making Teaching Community Property.* Washington, D.C.: American Association for Higher Education, 1996.

Jenkins, A., and Associates. "Teaching and Research: Student Perspectives and Policy Implications." *Studies in Higher Education,* June 1998, *23*(2), 127–141.

Jenkins, A., and Associates. *Reshaping Teaching in Higher Education: Linking Teaching and Research.* London: Kogan Page, 2002.

Kaster, G. "Teaching, Learning, and Thinking Historically." Unpublished grant proposal to Bush Foundation, Gustavus Adolphus College, Jan. 9, 2004.

Keller, F. S. "Good-bye, teacher. . . ." *Journal of Applied Behavior Analysis,* Jan. 1968, *1*(1), 79–89.

Kelly, T. M. "For Better or Worse? The Marriage of Web and Classroom." In P. Hutchings (ed.), *Opening Lines: Approaches to the Scholarship of Teaching and Learning*. Menlo Park, Calif.: The Carnegie Foundation for the Advancement of Teaching, 2000.

Kemmis, S., and McTaggart, R. "Participatory Action Research." In N. K. Denzin and Y. S. Lincoln (eds.), *Handbook of Qualitative Research* (2nd ed.). Thousand Oaks, Calif.: Sage, 2000.

Kernan, A. B. *In Plato's Cave*. New Haven, Conn.: Yale University Press, 1999.

Kimball, B. *Orators and Philosophers: A History of the Idea of Liberal Education*. New York: Teachers College Press, 1986.

Kimball, B. "Interpreting the Liberal Arts: Four Lectures on the History and Historiography of the Liberal Arts." *Liberal Arts: Journal of the Institute for the Liberal Arts at Westmont,* 2003, *1*(1), 3–52.

Knight Higher Education Collaborative. "Who Owns Teaching?" *Policy Perspectives,* Aug. 2002, *10*(4), 1–9.

Krathwohl, D. R., Bloom, B. S., and Masia, B. B. *Taxonomy of Educational Objectives: Affective Domain*. New York: David McKay, 1964.

Kreber, C. "Conceptualizing the Scholarship of Teaching and Identifying Unresolved Issues: The Framework for This Volume." In C. Kreber (ed.), *Revisiting Scholarship: Perspectives on the Scholarship of Teaching*. New Directions for Teaching and Learning, no. 86. San Francisco: Jossey-Bass, 2001.

Kreber, C. "Controversy and Consensus on the Scholarship of Teaching." *Studies in Higher Education,* May 2002, 27(2), 151–167.

Kreber, C. "Challenging the Dogma: Toward a More Inclusive View of the Scholarship of Teaching." *Journal on Excellence in College Teaching,* 2003, *14*(2-3): 27–43.

Kreber, C., and Cranton, P. A. "Exploring the Scholarship of Teaching." *Journal of Higher Education,* July-Aug. 2000, *71*(4), 476–496.

Laurillard, D. *Rethinking University Teaching: A Conversational Framework for the Effective Use of Learning Technologies* (2nd ed.). London: Routledge/Farmer, 2002.

Lessig, L. "Reclaiming a Commons." Keynote address at the Berkman Center's Building a Digital Commons Conference, Cambridge, Mass., May 20, 1999 (draft 1.01, June 21, 1999). http://www.cyber.law.harvard.edu/events/lessigkeynote.pdf. Accessed April 6, 2005.

Levine, A., and Cureton, J. S. "College Life: An Obituary." *Change,* May-June 1998, *30*(3), 12–17.

Light, R. J. *The Harvard Assessment Seminars: First Report. Explorations with Students and Faculty About Teaching, Learning, and Student Life.* Cambridge, Mass.: Harvard University, 1990.

Light, R. J. *The Harvard Assessment Seminars: Second Report. Explorations with Students and Faculty About Teaching, Learning, and Student Life.* Cambridge, Mass.: Harvard University, 1992.

Light, R. J. *Making the Most of College: Students Speak Their Minds.* Cambridge, Mass.: Harvard University Press, 2001.

Lindholm, J., Astin, A., Sax, L., and Korn, W. *The American College Teacher: National Norms for the 2001–02 HERI Faculty Survey.* Los Angeles: Higher Education Research Institute, University of California, 2002.

Linkon, S. "Students' Perspectives on Interdisciplinary Learning." In P. Hutchings (ed.), *Opening Lines: Approaches to the Scholarship of Teaching and Learning.* Menlo Park, Calif.: The Carnegie Foundation for the Advancement of Teaching, 2000.

Lowman, J. *Mastering the Techniques of Teaching.* San Francisco: Jossey-Bass, 1995.

Lueddeke, G. "Professionalising Teaching Practice in Higher Education: A Study on Disciplinary Variation and 'Teaching-Scholarship.' *Studies in Higher Education,* 2003, *28*(2), 213–228.

Lunsford, A. A. "Rethinking the Ph.D. in English." In C. Golde and G. Walker (eds.), *Envisioning the Future of Doctoral Education: Preparing Stewards of the Discipline.* San Francisco: Jossey-Bass, 2006.

McCormick, A. C. "Swirling and Double-Dipping: New Patterns of Student Attendance and Their Implications for Higher Education." In J. E. King, E. L. Anderson, M. E. Corrigan (eds.), *Changing Student Attendance Patterns: Challenges for Policy and Practice.* New Directions for Higher Education, no. 121. San Francisco: Jossey-Bass, 2003.

McKeachie, W. J. *McKeachie's Teaching Tips: Strategies, Research, and Theory for College and University Teachers.* Boston: Houghton Mifflin, 1999.

McSherry, C. *Who Owns Academic Work? Battling for Control of Academic Property.* Cambridge, Mass.: Harvard University Press, 2001.

Marchese, T. J. "The New Conversations About Learning: Insights from Neuroscience and Anthropology, Cognitive Science, and Work-Place Studies." In B. L. Cambridge (ed.), *Assessing Impact: Evidence and Action.* Washington, D.C.: American Association for Higher Education, 1997. http://www.aahe.org/pubs/TM-essay.htm. Accessed April 6, 2005.

Marcus, G. E. *Ethnography Through Thick and Thin.* Princeton, N.J.: Princeton University Press, 1998.

Margulies, A. H. "A New Model for Open Sharing." Paper presented at The Carnegie Foundation for The Advancement of Teaching, Stanford, Calif., Apr. 6, 2004.

Mathieu, R. D. "Teaching-as-Research: A Concept for Change at Research Universities," n.d. Madison: University of Wisconsin. http://www.solent.ac.uk/ExternalUP/318/bob_mathieu_s_paper.doc. Accessed April 6, 2005.

Merton, R. K. *On the Shoulders of Giants: A Shandean Postscript.* Chicago: University of Chicago Press, 1993.

Metzger, W. P. "The Academic Profession in the United States." In B. R. Clark (ed.), *The Academic Profession: National, Disciplinary, and Institutional Settings.* Berkeley: University of California Press, 1987.

Milford, L., Nelson, J., and Kleinsasser, A. *Warming Up the Chill.* Laramie: University of Wyoming Press, 2003.

Miller, M.A. "The Fund for the Improvement of Postsecondary Education: 30 Years of Making a Difference." *Change,* Sept.-Oct. 2002, *34*(5), 4.

Mills, D., and Huber, M. T. "Anthropology and the Educational 'Trading Zone': Disciplinarity, Pedagogy, and Professionalism." *Arts and Humanities in Higher Education,* Jan. 2005, *4*(1), 5–28.

MIT OpenCourseWare. *MIT OpenCourseWare Program Evaluation Findings: Summary Report.* Mar. 2004. http://ocw.mit.edu/OcwWeb/Global/AboutOCW/evaluation.htm. Accessed April 6, 2005.

Morreale, S. P., Applegate, J. L., Wulff, D. H., and Sprague, J. "The Scholarship of Teaching and Learning in Communication Studies, and Communication Scholarship in the Process of Teaching and Learning." In M. T. Huber and S. P. Morreale (eds.), *Disciplinary Styles in the Scholarship of Teaching and Learning: Exploring Common Ground.* Washington, D.C.: American Association for Higher Education and The Carnegie Foundation for the Advancement of Teaching, 2002.

Muramatsu, B., and Agogino, A. M. "The National Engineering Education Delivery System: A Digital Library for Engineering Education." *D-Lib Magazine,* Apr. 1999, *5*(4), 1–14. http://www.dlib.org/dlib/april99/muramatsu/04muramatsu.html. Accessed April 6, 2005.

Narayan, R. K. *The English Teacher.* London: Eyre and Spottiswoode, 1945.

National Academy of Education. *Recommendations Regarding Research Priorities: An Advisory Report to the National Educational Research Policy and Priorities Board.* Washington, D.C.: National Academy of Education, 1999.

National Center for Postsecondary Improvement. *Beyond Dead Reckoning: Research Priorities for Redirecting American Higher Education.* Stanford, Calif.: National Center for Postsecondary Improvement, Stanford University, 2002.

National Center for Public Policy in Higher Education. *About Measuring Up: Questions and Answers About Measuring Up.* http://measuringup.highereducation.org/qa.cfm. 2004. Accessed April 6, 2005.

National Research Council. *Moving Beyond Myths: Revitalizing Undergraduate Mathematics.* Washington, D.C.: National Academy Press, 1991.

National Research Council. *Engineering Education: Designing an Adaptive System.* Washington, D.C.: National Academy Press, 1995a.

National Research Council. *Reshaping the Graduate Education of Scientists and Engineers.* Washington, D.C.: National Academy Press, 1995b.

National Research Council. *From Analysis to Action: Undergraduate Education in Science, Mathematics, Engineering, and Technology. Report of a Convocation.* Washington, D.C.: National Academy Press, 1996a.

National Research Council. *The Role of Scientists in the Professional Development of Science Teachers.* Washington, D.C.: National Academy Press, 1996b.

National Research Council. *Science Teacher Preparation in an Era of Standards-Based Reform.* Washington, D.C.: National Academy Press, 1997.

National Research Council. *Transforming Undergraduate Education in Science, Mathematics, Engineering, and Technology.* Washington, D.C.: National Academy Press, 1999.

National Research Council. *Educating Teachers of Science, Mathematics, and Technology: New Practices for the New Millennium.* Washington, D.C.: National Academy Press, 2000a.

National Research Council. *Enhancing the Postdoctoral Experience for Scientists and Engineers: A Guide for Postdoctoral Scholars, Advisors, Institutions, Funding Organizations, and Disciplinary Societies.* Washington, D.C.: National Academy Press, 2000b.

National Research Council. *Scientific Research in Education.* Committee on Scientific Principles for Education Research. R. J. Shavelson and L. Towne (eds.). Center for Education, Division of Behavioral and Social Sciences and Education. Washington, D.C.: National Academy Press, 2002.

Nelson, J., and Kleinsasser, A. "Mutual Benefits, Continuing Challenges." In B. Cambridge (ed.), *Campus Progress: Supporting the Scholarship of Teaching and Learning.* Washington, D.C.: American Association for Higher Education, 2004.

Nowotny, H., Scott, P., and Gibbons, M. *Re-Thinking Science: Knowledge and the Public in an Age of Uncertainty.* Cambridge, England: Polity Press, 2001.

Nummedal, S. G., Benson, J. B., and Chew, S. L. "Disciplinary Styles in the Scholarship of Teaching: A View from Psychology." In M. T. Huber and S. Morreale (eds.), *Disciplinary Styles in the Scholarship of Teaching and Learning: Exploring Common Ground.* Washington, D.C.: American Association for Higher Education and The Carnegie Foundation for the Advancement of Teaching, 2002.

O'Meara, K. "Effects of Encouraging Multiple Forms of Scholarship Nationwide and Across Institutional Types." In K. O'Meara and R. E. Rice (eds.), *Faculty Priorities Reconsidered: Rewarding Multiple Forms of Scholarship.* Jossey-Bass with the American Association for Higher Education, 2005.

Orrill, R. (ed.). *Education and Democracy: Re-Imagining Liberal Learning in America.* New York: College Board, 1997.

Ostroff, W. "Raising Metacognitive Awareness Increases Student Responsibility for Learning Process." Carnegie Academy for the Scholarship of Teaching and Learning (CASTL) Electronic Workspace. Stanford, Calif.: The Carnegie Foundation for the Advancement of Teaching, June 2004. http://kml2.carnegiefoundation.org/html/poster.php?id=521. Accessed April 6, 2005.

Ottenhoff, J. "Digital Culture and the Future of Liberal Education." Paper presented at the Annual Meeting of the Association of American Colleges and Universities, Washington, D.C., Jan. 24, 2004.

Owen-Smith, P. "What Is Cognitive-Affective Learning (CAL)?" *Journal of Cognitive Affective Learning,* Fall 2004, *1*(1), 11. http://www.jcal.emory.edu/. Accessed April 6, 2005.

Pace, D. "The Amateur in the Operating Room: History and the Scholarship of Teaching and Learning." *American Historical Review,* Oct. 2004, *109*(4), 1171–1192.

Palmer, P. J. "Divided No More: A Movement Approach to Educational Reform." *Change,* Mar.-Apr. 1992, *24*(2), 10–17.

Palmer, P. J. *The Courage to Teach: Exploring the Inner Landscape of a Teacher's Life.* San Francisco: Jossey-Bass, 1998.

Passmore, J. A. *The Philosophy of Teaching.* London: Duckworth, 1980.

"Peer Review of Teaching Project." http://www.unl.edu/peerrev/. Accessed April 6, 2005.

Perry, W. G., Jr. *Forms of Ethical and Intellectual Development in the College Years: A Scheme.* San Francisco: Jossey-Bass, 1998. (Originally published 1970.)

Phillips, M. T. "A Case Study of Theory, Voice, Pedagogy, and Joy." In P. Hutchings (ed.), *Opening Lines: Approaches to the Scholarship of Teaching and Learning.* Menlo Park, Calif.: The Carnegie Foundation for the Advancement of Teaching, 2000.

Pingree, A. "The Role of Teaching and Learning Centers in Peer Review: Opportunities and Challenges." Paper presented at the Conference on Making Learning Visible: Peer Review and the Scholarship of Teaching, University of Nebraska, Lincoln, Mar. 27, 2004.

Purves, A. C. *The Idea of Difficulty in Literature.* Albany: State University of New York, 1991.

Quinlan, K. M. "About Teaching and Learning Centers," *AAHE Bulletin,* Oct. 1991, *44*(2), 11–16.

Ramsden, P. *Learning to Teach in Higher Education.* New York: Routledge, 1992.

Randall, N. "Navigating the Scholarship of Teaching and Learning." In B. L. Cambridge (ed.), *Campus Progress: Supporting the Scholarship of Teaching and Learning.* Washington, D.C.: American Association for Higher Education, 2004.

Ransom, J. C. *The New Criticism.* Norfolk, Conn.: New Directions, 1941.

Reuben, J. A. *The Making of the Modern University: Intellectual Transformation and the Marginalization of Morality.* Chicago: The University of Chicago Press, 1996.

Rhem, J. "Editor's Note." *National Teaching and Learning Forum,* Mar. 2003, *12*(6), 3.

Rice, R. E. "Towards a Broader Conception of Scholarship: The American Context." In T. G. Whiston and R. L. Geiger (eds.), *Research and Higher Education: The United Kingdom and the United States.* Milton Keynes, England: Open University Press, 1991.

Rice, R. E. "Welcome to the Conference!" In program for the AAHE Conference on Faculty Roles & Rewards, "From 'My Work' to 'Our Work': Realigning Faculty Work with College and University Purposes," Phoenix, Jan. 19–22, 1995.

Richlin, L. "Scholarly Teaching and the Scholarship of Teaching." In C. Kreber (ed.), *Revisiting Scholarship: Perspectives on the Scholarship of Teaching.* New Directions for Teaching and Learning, no. 86. San Francisco: Jossey-Bass, 2001.

Richlin, L. "Understanding, Promoting, and Operationalizing the Scholarship of Teaching and Learning." *Journal on Excellence in College Teaching,* 2003, *14*(2–3), 1–4.

Root-Bernstein, R. S., and Root-Bernstein, M. "Learning to Think with Emotion." *Chronicle of Higher Education,* Jan. 14, 2000, *46*(19), A64.

Rosovsky, H., and Hartley, M. *Evaluation and the Academy: Are We Doing the Right Thing?* Cambridge, Mass.: American Academy of Arts and Sciences, 2002.

Rothblatt, S. *Living Arts: Comparative and Historical Perspectives on Liberal Education.* Washington, D.C.: Association of American Colleges and Universities, 2003.

Rudolph, F. *Curriculum: A History of the American Undergraduate Course of Study Since 1636.* San Francisco: Jossey-Bass, 1977.

Sabral, D. T. "Improving Learning Skills: A Self-Help Group Approach." *Higher Education,* Jan. 1997, *33*(1), 39–50.

Salvatori, M. R. "Towards a Hermeneutics of Difficulty." In L. Z. Smith (ed.), *Audits of Meaning.* Portsmouth, N.H.: Boynton/Cook Heineman, 1988.

Salvatori, M. R. "Difficulty: The Great Educational Divide." In P. Hutchings (ed.), *Opening Lines: Approaches to the Scholarship of Teaching and Learning.* Menlo Park, Calif.: The Carnegie Foundation for the Advancement of Teaching, 2000.

Salvatori, M. R. "The Scholarship of Teaching: Beyond the Anecdotal." *Pedagogy,* Fall 2002, *2*(3), 297–310.

Salvatori, M. R., and Donahue, P. "English Studies in the Scholarship of Teaching." In M. T. Huber and S. P. Morreale (eds.), *Disciplinary Styles in the Scholarship of Teaching and Learning: Exploring Common Ground.* Washington, D.C.: American Association for Higher Education and The Carnegie Foundation for the Advancement of Teaching, 2002.

Salvatori, M. R., and Donahue, P. *The Elements (and Pleasures) of Difficulty.* New York: Pearson/Longman, 2004.

Sax, L., Astin, A., Arredondo, M., and Korn, W. *The American College Teacher: National Norms for the 1995–96 HERI Faculty Survey.* Los Angeles, Calif.: Higher Education Research Institute, University of California, 1996.

Scheinberg, C. "Cognitive Apprenticeship as Pedagogical Strategy: Introducing Conversacolor." *National Teaching and Learning Forum,* Oct. 2003, *12*(6), 1–2, 4.

Schneider, C. G., and Schoenberg, R. "Habits Hard to Break: How Persistent Features of Campus Life Frustrate Curricular Reform." *Change,* Mar.-Apr. 1999, *31*(2), 30–35.

Schoenfeld, A. C., and Magnan, R. *Mentor in a Manual: Climbing the Academic Ladder to Tenure.* Madison, Wisc.: Magna Publications, 1994.

Schön, D. A. *The Reflective Practitioner: How Professionals Think in Action.* New York: Basic Books, 1983.

Schön, D. A. "The New Scholarship Requires a New Epistemology." *Change,* Nov.-Dec. 1995, *27*(6), 26–34.

Schwab, J. "Structure of the Disciplines." In G. W. Ford and L. Pugno (eds.), *The Structure of Knowledge and the Curriculum.* Skokie, Ill.: Rand McNally, 1964.

Seldin, P. *The Teaching Portfolio: A Practical Guide to Improved Performance and Promotion/Tenure Decisions.* Bolton, Mass.: Anker, 1997.

Seymour, E. "Tracking the Processes of Change in U.S. Undergraduate Education in Science, Mathematics, Engineering, and Technology." *Science Education,* Jan. 2002, *86*(1), 79–105.

Seymour, E., and Hewitt, N. M. *Talking About Leaving: Why Undergraduates Leave the Sciences*. Boulder, Colo.: Westview Press, 1997.

Shavelson, R., and Huang, L. "Responding Responsibly to the Frenzy to Assess Learning in Higher Education." *Change*, Jan.-Feb. 2003, *35*(1), 10–19.

Shenk, G. E. Final oral report. Carnegie Academy for the Scholarship of Teaching and Learning (CASTL). Menlo Park, Calif.: The Carnegie Foundation for the Advancement of Teaching, June 2001a.

Shenk, G. E. "Sharing Researchable Problems in the Scholarship of Teaching and Learning: History and Civic Participation." Paper presented at the First Annual Joint United Kingdom and United States Conference on the Scholarship of Teaching and Learning, Kensington Town Hall, London, England, June 6, 2001b.

Shenk, G. E., and Takacs, D. "Historically Informed Political Project (HIPP)." (From class syllabus for Social and Political History of California, SBSC/ESSP). Seaside, Calif.: California State University-Monterey Bay, Fall 2000.

Shenk, G. E., and Takacs, D. "History and Civic Participation: An Example of the Scholarship of Teaching and Learning." *AHA Perspectives*, Apr. 2002, *40*(4). http://www.historians.org/perspectives/issues/2002/0204/0204teach2.htm. Accessed April 6, 2005.

Showalter, E. "The Risks of Good Teaching: How One Professor and Nine TAs Plunged into Pedagogy." *Chronicle of Higher Education*, July 9, 1999, *45*(44), B4-B6.

Shulman, L. S. "Knowledge and Teaching: Foundations of the New Reform." *Harvard Educational Review*, Feb. 1987, *57*(1), 1–22.

Shulman, L. S. "Teaching as Community Property: Putting an End to Pedagogical Solitude." *Change*, Nov.-Dec. 1993, *25*(6), 6–7.

Shulman, L. S. "Course Anatomy: The Dissection and Analysis of Knowledge Through Teaching." In P. Hutchings (ed.), *The Course Portfolio: How Faculty Can Examine Their Teaching to Advance Practice and Improve Student Learning*. Washington, D.C.: American Association for Higher Education, 1998.

Shulman, L. S. "Taking Learning Seriously." *Change*, July-Aug. 1999, *31*(4), 10–17.

Shulman, L. S. "From Minsk to Pinsk: Why a Scholarship of Teaching and Learning?" *Journal of Scholarship of Teaching and Learning*, 2000a, *1*(1), 48–51. http://www.carnegiefoundation.org/CASTL/highered/resources.htm. Accessed April 12, 2005.

Shulman, L. S. "Inventing the Future." In P. Hutchings (ed.), *Opening Lines: Approaches to the Scholarship of Teaching and Learning*. Menlo Park, Calif.: The Carnegie Foundation for the Advancement of Teaching, 2000b.

Shulman, L. S. "Foreword." In P. Hutchings (ed.), *Ethics of Inquiry: Issues in the Scholarship of Teaching and Learning.* Menlo Park, Calif.: The Carnegie Foundation for the Advancement of Teaching, 2002a.

Shulman, L. S. "Making Differences: A Table of Learning." *Change,* Nov.-Dec. 2002b, *34*(6), 36–44.

Shulman, L. S. "Lamarck's Revenge: Teaching Among the Scholarships." In P. Hutchings (ed.), *Teaching as Community Property: Essays on Higher Education.* San Francisco: Jossey-Bass, 2004a.

Shulman, L. S. "The Wisdom of Practice: Managing Complexity in Medicine and Teaching." In S. Wilson (ed.), *The Wisdom of Practice: Essays on Teaching, Learning, and Learning to Teach.* San Francisco: Jossey-Bass, 2004b. (Originally published 1987.)

Shulman, L. S. "Visions of the Possible: Models for Campus Support of the Scholarship of Teaching and Learning." In P. Hutchings (ed.), *Teaching as Community Property: Essays on Higher Education.* San Francisco: Jossey-Bass, 2004c.

Skogsberg, E. Panel presentation at the American Association for Higher Education Summer Academy, Stowe, Vt., July 17, 2004.

Sperling, C. B. "How Community Colleges Understand the Scholarship of Teaching and Learning." *Community College Journal of Research and Practice,* Aug. 2003, *27*(1), 593–601.

Steiner, G. *On Difficulty and Other Essays.* New York: Oxford University Press, 1978.

Subject Network for Sociology, Anthropology, and Politic Science. "Sharing Ideas and Research in Social Sciences Learning and Teaching," n.d. http://www.c-sap.bham.ac.uk/. Accessed April 6, 2005.

Sullivan, W. M. "A Life of the Mind for Practice: Professional Education and the Liberal Arts." Menlo Park, Calif.: The Carnegie Foundation for the Advancement of Teaching, 2002. http://www.carnegiefoundation.org/PPP/seminar.htm. Accessed April 6, 2005.

Takacs, D. "Using Student Work as Evidence." In P. Hutchings (ed.), *Ethics of Inquiry: Issues in the Scholarship of Teaching and Learning.* Menlo Park, Calif.: The Carnegie Foundation for the Advancement of Teaching, 2002.

Taylor, I., and Burgess, H. "Orientation to Self-Directed Learning: Paradox Nor Paradigm." *Studies in Higher Education,* Mar. 1995, *20*(1), 87–99.

Tobias, S. *They're Not Dumb, They're Different: Stalking the Second Tier.* Tucson, Ariz.: The Research Corporation, 1990.

Tompkins, J. P. *A Life in School: What the Teacher Learned.* Redding, Mass.: Perseus, 1996.

Trigwell, K. "Student Learning and the Scholarship of Teaching/Learning." Keynote speech at the International Society for the Scholarship of Teaching and Learning Inaugural Conference, Indiana University, Bloomington, Oct. 21, 2004.

Trigwell, K., Martin, E., Benjamin, J., and Prosser, M. "Scholarship of Teaching: A Model." *Higher Education Research and Development,* July 2000, *19*(2), 155–168.

United States Bureau of the Census. *Historical Statistics of the United States, Part 2.* Washington, D.C.: United States Bureau of the Census, 1975.

Vess, D., and Linkon, S. "Navigating the Interdisciplinary Archipelago: The Scholarship of Interdisciplinary Teaching and Learning." In M. T. Huber and S. P. Morreale (eds.), *Disciplinary Styles in the Scholarship of Teaching and Learning: Exploring Common Ground.* Washington, D.C.: American Association for Higher Education and The Carnegie Foundation for the Advancement of Teaching, 2002.

Walvoord, B. E. "Building on Each Others' Work: Uses and Audiences for the 'Public' Scholarship of Teaching." Unpublished manuscript. South Bend, Ind.: University of Notre Dame, Mar. 2000.

Wankat, P. C., Felder, R. M., Smith, K. A., and Oreovicz, F. S. "The Scholarship of Teaching and Learning in Engineering." In M. T. Huber and S. P. Morreale (eds.), *Disciplinary Styles in the Scholarship of Teaching and Learning: Exploring Common Ground.* Washington, D.C.: American Association for Higher Education and The Carnegie Foundation for the Advancement of Teaching, 2002.

Werder, C. "What Matters Over Time: Documenting Student Learning." In B. Cambridge (ed.), *Campus Progress: Supporting the Scholarship of Teaching and Learning.* Washington, D.C.: American Association for Higher Education, 2004.

Werder, C., Redmond, P. J., Purdue, J., and Patrick, K. "Creating a Reflective Space: The Teaching and Learning Academy at Western Washington University." *Washington Center for Improving the Quality of Undergraduate Education Newsletter,* Fall 2003, 38–40.

Wineburg, S. S. *Historical Thinking and Other Unnatural Acts: Charting the Future of Teaching the Past.* Philadelphia, Pa.: Temple University Press, 2001.

Wright, S. "C-SAP's Approach in a Context of Change." Unpublished manuscript. Centre for Learning and Teaching in Sociology, Anthropology and Politics (C-SAP), University of Birmingham, Birmingham, United Kingdom, Mar. 2003.

Yancey, K. B. *Reflection in the Writing Classroom.* Logan: Utah State University Press, 1998.

Zemsky, R., and Massy, W. *Thwarted Innovation: What Happened to e-learning and Why.* Philadelphia: Learning Alliance of the University of Pennsylvania, 2004.

INDEX

A

B

I

J

K

L

N

O

P

Q

R

S

U

V

W

Y

Z